Pedaling on the North Coast

15   14   13   12   11   5   4   3   2   1

ISBN 978-1-931968-96-6 (paperback)
LCCN 2011923679

The paper used in this publication meets the minimum requirements of American National
Standard for Information Sciences—Permanence of Paper for Printed Library Materials, ANSI
Z39.48–1984. ∞

Bike illustration on cover and chapter pages by Lan X. Le. Cover and interior design by Amy
Freels. *Pedaling on the North Coast* was typeset in Minion and Frutiger, printed on sixty-pound
natural, and bound by BookMasters of Ashland, Ohio.

Pedaling on the North Coast

Biking the Streets of Greater Cleveland

Stan Purdum
and Murray Fishel

Curt Brown
RESEARCH ASSISTANT

RINGTAW BOOKS
AKRON, OHIO

In memory of Judy Fishel, whose encouragement led to me to create these routes.
—Murray

To Jeanine, for cheering me on.
—Stan

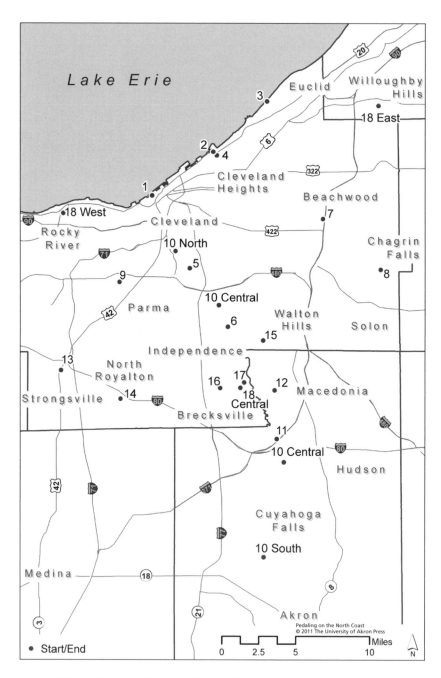

Eighteen rides around Northeast Ohio. Numbers correspond to the ride number.

Contents

Acknowledgments

Our thanks to Tom Nezovich, Dave Pulliam and Marty Cooperman, who shared their knowledge of where to bike in Greater Cleveland, thereby improving the routes in this book. Tom and Dave, along with Wayne Ostrander, Scott Purdum, and Ken Johnson made riding these routes even more fun by pedaling several of them with us.

We are grateful to the staff of the University of Akron Press: to Curt Brown for his conscientious editing of the book; to Amy Freels for her attractive layout and design work; to Paul Stephenson for his map-making; to Zac Bettendorf, Michael Goroff, and Abby Thompson for their proofreading; to Julie Gammon for her nonstop marketing efforts; to Carol Slatter for her careful attention to the manufacturing of the volume; and to Director Tom Bacher, who saw the vision and green-lighted the project.

Introduction

Stan Purdum

From 1919 until the mid 1950s, Cleveland was the home of the Murray Ohio Manufacturing Company, which made, among other things, bicycles for the youth market. Cleveland was also the home of Murray Fishel's family. So when his father went looking for a bicycle for Murray's sixth birthday, it was no surprise he came home with a Murray. The next morning, the birthday boy came downstairs and was thrilled to find that not only had his parents gotten him a bike, but also that they had even specially named it for him!

Murray's early love affair with cycling ended the day he got his driver's license, but it was reborn in 1991, as he planned his retirement from Kent State University's Department of Political Science. He wanted to concentrate on his consulting business, but knew that business wouldn't occupy him full time, and several retired friends had stressed the importance of having something to do. So Murray bought a bicycle and has been riding ever since, wearing out several bikes and pedaling well over a hundred thousand miles.

Good thing he kept riding, because according to his doctor, cycling later saved his life.

Although all that cycling has kept a rosy glow on Murray's cheeks and a spring in his step, other factors—specifically his genetic disposition toward high cholesterol—resulted in his having a heart attack late in his seventh decade. His cardiologist installed a stent in one of his arteries, but told Murray that had he not been so physically fit from cycling, the attack would have killed him. He was so fit, in fact, that only a small portion of his heart was damaged, and after treatment, he was able to return to cycling.

I met Murray on a ride with a group of mostly retired men who meet weekly for a bicycle trek to lunch, pedaling to a different restaurant each time. Appropriately, they have dubbed their association "The ROMEOS" (Retired Old Men Eating Out). I'm not retired, but a member had seen an article about my book of bike rides in Northeast Ohio, *Pedaling to Lunch*, and invited me to join the group for one of their jaunts. Along the way, I fell in beside a member who introduced himself as Murray Fishel. Murray said he lived in the Cleveland area and asked why I hadn't included many Greater Cleveland rides in my book. I explained that I hadn't because, living in North Canton, I didn't know Cleveland very well.

As we continued pedaling and talking, we found that we both had ridden cross-nation tours, had both enjoyed numerous other cycling adventures, and generally had a lot in common. Then Murray mentioned that he enjoyed plotting bicycle routes throughout Greater Cleveland and often led rides for acquaintances in and around the city. "Maybe you could do a book of Cleveland rides someday," Murray said.

"Maybe I could," I said, "if you did the routing."

You are holding the result in your hands. This book is a cooperative venture with Murray. He laid out the routes, the two of us—often in the company of friends—rode them together, I wrote about our experiences, and Murray reviewed what I had written and suggested additions and improvements. I'm delighted that several of Murray's rides, captured in this book, will be part of his legacy to the Greater Cleveland cycling community.

Along the way, Murray and I have become not only cycling and publishing partners, but good friends as well. We've each made other new friends in the process. Murray brought two of his cycling pals to several of the rides—Cleveland native Tom Nezovich and long-time Cleveland area resident Dave Pulliam. I brought two of my riding buddies, Wayne Ostrander from Suffield and my brother Scott Purdum, who lives in Ravenna. Sharing the fellowship of these self-propelled journeys, it didn't take long for us to become a cohesive group.

In the ride narrations, I've mentioned the bicycles we rode. "Bicycle people" tend not so much to replace their steeds, as to add new ones to their stable. Tom, for example, owns more bikes than anyone else I know. Murray owns four, Dave owns three, Wayne and I both own two, and Scott owned two until a mishap damaged one beyond repair. So if, as you read the chapters, you notice that we're not always on the same bikes, that's the reason. But that's not to suggest that you need special or multiple bicycles to ride these routes; any geared bike in good, working order is sufficient.

A word about the routing: As you ride these routes, you'll notice we've used a few roads in more than one ride, and there's a good reason for that. Not all streets and roads in Greater Cleveland are bike friendly. Thus, a few rides include the same portion of Twinsburg Road because it offers one of the few safe ways to cross the State Route 8 high-speed four-lane. Likewise, Lakeshore Boulevard, Valley Parkway, and Riverview Road each make more than one appearance because they lend themselves well to cycling. Each ride is its own adventure, however, and we've designed the rides with that in mind.

Murray and I are happy to provide these routes for your exercise, exploration, enjoyment, and exhilaration. Happy riding.

Introduction

Murray Fishel

Stan is a twenty-first century Renaissance man. Some people have one career and aren't happy in what they do. Stan has one career and is happy, but has never been satisfied with just that alone. He's been able to build his life around family, church, language, bicycling, and travel. And, it really is pretty remarkable that he's able to give each of these the dedication that many struggle with when only pursuing one!

I first learned of Stan when I saw his book *Pedaling to Lunch* in a local bookstore. I won't repeat the subsequent chain of events that led to our collaboration on this book, as it isn't important here. What is important is that we were drawn together by our love of bicycling and an intense interest in sharing that pleasure with others.

Stan and I share certain common beliefs. First, we both believe in the slogan, "Ride to Eat." Second, we both know that we see things from our bike saddles that we would never see anywhere else. Third, we are firm believers that bicycling is vital to our mental and physical fitness. And, finally, we both love to share our rides with others and write about bicycling.

Stan and I differ in opinion on certain things as well. Stan likes hills. I like down hills. Stan only counts hills if he has to use his granny gear. I count hills if there's a half-percent grade. You can really get some insight into Stan from an exchange we had recently on *Pedaling to Lunch's* "Stark Reality" ride in Stark County:

Me: *"How many hills are there before lunch?"*
Stan: *"Four."*
Me: *"Great. I can do that. After all, it's seventeen miles to lunch."*

As we roll along, I notice a large hill rising in front of me.

Stan: *"Here's the first hill."*
Me: *(under my breath) "But this is the* FIFTH *hill by my count."*

Ah, I guess the perception of reality is more important than the reality itself. Our perceptions are quite different, but that's what makes this book appropriate for cyclists of all skills. For each ride you get both of our "realities."

Stan provides you insights and challenges. I provide the streets and restaurants. There's plenty for any cyclist to love, there's plenty to challenge, and you'll never go hungry!

Before You Ride

Cycling is fun. Unless you want to become a professional cyclist, weekend riding doesn't require a lot of expensive or fancy equipment, and almost anybody in reasonable health can pedal around. The following advice will make your cycling safer, more enjoyable, and more comfortable.

Safety

Always wear a helmet. While falls are not common, a good-quality helmet will spare you serious head injury. Several years ago, I was rolling downhill on a country road when my map suddenly blew out of my front pouch. Without thought, I hit the brakes hard to stop and retrieve it. I flew over the handlebars and tumbled several times on the gravel of the road's shoulder. My bike ended up with bent handlebars and a damaged rear wheel. I got a pulled thigh muscle, numerous cuts, scrapes, abrasions, and bent glasses. My head, however, was okay, but only because the helmet took the blow—a blow so hard that my helmet split. It "died" and I didn't. I was sore, but I was able to straighten the bent wheel and ride home.

I also suggest using a flashing taillight on overcast days and after dark. A headlight is a good accessory, too. Many of these and other items are reviewed in *Bicycling* (www.bicycling.com).

Mechanical Problems

Being prepared for minor mechanical problems will make your day of riding more enjoyable. If you keep your bike properly maintained to begin with, you are unlikely to have any problems major enough to derail your ride. And unlike a car, most of the things that can go wrong mechanically on a bike do not actually prevent you from continuing your journey. A broken spoke or two, a squeaky bearing, or even a broken shift-cable will rarely force you to stop. However, a flat tire will, literally, deflate your progress.

To prevent tire trouble, start out with good tires inflated to the pressure recommended on the tire itself. Since flats can occur nonetheless, I carry a spare inner tube, a set of three tire levers (the "spoon-shaped" tools for removing a tire from the rim to install the new tube), and a small air pump that mounts to my bike frame. (Alternatively, you can use a CO_2 cartridge system for re-inflating the tire.) Since my wheels can be removed from the frame by opening quick-release levers (a common feature on most newer bikes), I need no other tools for dealing with a flat. If your wheels are attached to the frame with axle nuts, you'll have to carry the appropriate-sized wrench to remove the wheel.

Additionally, I carry a small combination Allen wrench (hex key) set that enables me to adjust any bolt on the bike, though I seldom have to use it. I also take along a chain-breaker tool for chain repairs, though I don't consider that essential for most riders. In the unlikely event of a broken chain, your best recourse may be to use your cell phone to call a friend for a ride. All of these tools come in small combination sets that can be found at bicycle shops.

Clothing

Prior to riding, I usually check the local forecast so I am aware of the temperature, wind speed and direction, and amount of sun I will encounter. This allows me to dress appropriately and avoid taking extra layers of clothing. If the weather conditions will be changing, I might have to take off one layer or bring an additional layer.

I recommend bicycle shorts for all rides (under other layers on cold days), but in warm and dry weather, you can get away with T-shirts and other everyday garments. Many riders don't cycle in colder weather, but if you do, it is wise to dress in layers and wear clothing made of the performance fabrics that wick moisture away from your body. The standard advice for cold weather riding is to think in terms of three layers: a base layer of wicking fabric, a middle layer of insulating fabric, and an outer layer of wind-breaking fabric. That advice is fine as far as it goes, but in practice, it is not precise enough to ensure comfort at different temperatures. Depending on the temperature, you may need to don two or three insulating layers between the base layer and the outer layer.

The best way to determine what you need to wear on cooler days is trial-and-error coupled with a little record keeping. Trial-and-error is not difficult if you have some arrangement on your bike to stash extra clothing, such as a rack, a pouch, or a saddlebag. Then just take a bit more clothing than you think you are likely to need and see what actually keeps you comfortable. Unless your memory is exceptional, however, the key is to keep a written record of the temperature and the required number of layers. In my experience, for every five degrees the temperature drops below 65, I need to add a piece of clothing—long sleeves, gloves, a skull cap, an additional pair of socks, etc.

Comfort

The single most important item for comfort on long rides is a properly fitted saddle. Fit is far more important than padding. You can find saddles that feature lots of padding and that feel great for short neighborhood rides. But on longer hauls, the padding compresses and doesn't feel nearly as good. Saddles come in different widths, different material, and are structured differently for men and women. You might need to experiment with a few saddles, and some bike shops even have loaner saddles you can try. Personally, I've found that the classic leather saddle works best for me.

After you've chosen a saddle, have it properly adjusted. A professional at a local bike shop can do this for you, or you can also find instructions on the Internet or in your bicycle user's manual. Saddles need to be set for the proper height, tilt, and distance from your handlebars. You can find information on choosing and adjusting saddles at www.bicycling.com and other websites.

To stay comfortable during your ride, buy bicycle shorts. Shorts are important because they have a little padding, provide support, and are designed to reduce friction, rubbing, and to wick away moisture. Follow the manufacturer's instruction on proper care.

Take at least two water bottles on rides. I usually fill one with a sports drink. I also carry an energy bar because cycling burns lots of calories. In hot weather, I take along pretzels to replenish my body's sodium level.

With attention to these few matters, you are all set for great adventures on northeast Ohio's byways.

Here are a few websites to check out:

Adventure Cycling Association
www.adventurecycling.org

League of American Bicyclists
www.bikeleague.org

Ohio Department of Transportation
www2.dot.state.oh.us/bike

Pedestrian and Bicycling Information Center
www.bicyclinginfo.org

Sheldon Brown's Bicycle Technical Info
sheldonbrown.com

Ride 1
Lake Parks West

Route: Wendy Park to Huntington Reservation
Distance: 29 miles
Terrain: Flat
Communities Visited: Cleveland, Lakewood, Rocky River,
   Bay Village
Starting/Ending Point: Wendy Park on Whiskey Island
Points of Interest: Wendy Park, Edgewater Beach and
   State Park, Lakewood Park, Rocky River Park, Bradstreet
   Landing, Huntington Reservation, closed Coast Guard
   station, spectacular view of the Cleveland skyline, beautiful
   houses
How to Get There: Follow State Route 2 (SR2) west
   (Memorial Shoreway) to Edgewater Beach and Park exit.
   Make two quick right turns at bottom of ramp, which puts
   you on (unmarked) Island Drive, and follow signs for
   Whiskey Island, Wendy Park, and the Coast Guard station.
   At the "Y" that splits around a parking area, take the right fork.

Cleveland and the surrounding region are full of appealing sights and intriguing locations, but the single largest natural asset is the proximity to the eleventh largest lake in the world, Lake Erie. This ride provides an opportunity to enjoy the beautiful western portion of the lake, see stunning views of the Cleveland skyline, and pedal past some compelling shoreline homes.

The ride starts at the historic, but now closed, U.S. Coast Guard Station at the mouth of the Cuyahoga River. At the other end of the route is the Huntington Reservation, one of the jewels of the Cleveland Metroparks system. In between, the ride travels through or by four parks on the lake's edge, as well as through an assortment of attractive lakeside neighborhoods.

Changing Gears

There are many parks along the Lake Erie shoreline in the greater Cleveland area. Some belong to local communities, one is a Cleveland Metropark and six, including Edgewater Park, are units of the Cleveland Lakefront State Park system. The Lakefront Trail East ride visits four of the others and passes by the fifth. Those five are Wildwood Park, Villa Angela, Euclid Beach, Gordon Park, and the E. 55th Street Marina.

Unlike many of the rides in this book, which are loops, this one is mostly an "out-and-back" journey, and for good reason: we wanted to keep you near the water. There is a loop on the western end of the ride that puts you on a less busy road, but most of the ride is near the lake. In fact, with just a few exceptions, this ride sticks to the roads nearest the water's edge.

As mentioned in the introduction, part of the fun of these bicycle rides is eating somewhere new, and Murray and I and our riding buddies seldom miss an opportunity to do that. While there are a couple of chain restaurants directly on the return route, there are more interesting choices in both Rocky River and at Gordon Square. The latter is just a short excursion from the end of the route.

Murray and I, along with Tom and Dave, pick a comfortable, sunny day in April for this ride. In two vehicles, we enter Whiskey Island from Memorial Shoreway. Despite the name, this land was never actually an island, at least not in recorded history. When the first Europeans arrived, it was a small peninsula, bounded on the north by Lake Erie and on the south and west by the Cuyahoga River; it joined the mainland on the east. In 1827, however, the mouth of Cuyahoga River was rechanneled and directly connected with Lake Erie, removing the river's last two natural turns. After the original mouth was closed, the peninsula was reversed; it now joined the mainland on the west and was severed from it on the east by the new channel. The "Whiskey" part of the name came because a distillery occupied the land in the 1830s.

Murray leads the way eastward along the (unmarked) Island Drive toward the Whiskey Island Marina and beyond it at the northeastern end of the peninsula to Wendy Park. After the blacktop runs out, we continue on the gravel drive to the parking area at the end, near the entrance path to the old Coast Guard station (though we can't see it yet). We park and unload the bikes. Murray is riding his Bruce Gordon BLT touring bike. Dave is mounted on a Schwinn Range Searcher, a hybrid he recently bought on Craigslist. I'm riding my Specialized Sequoia Elite, a lightweight road bike. Tom is on his Trek 830 Antelope mountain bike, but equipped with road tires and "moustache" handlebars, which gives it a unique look and enables him to sit in a more upright position, the better to see city traffic.

Before setting out, we pedal on the short gravel path and then ride the seawall to the Coast Guard station at its end, where the Cuyahoga River empties into the lake at its rechanneled location. The Coast Guard station was designed by Cleveland architect J. Milton Dyer (who also designed City Hall) and constructed in 1940. It was listed on the National Register of Historic Places in 1976 and abandoned by the Coast Guard the same year. The building has deteriorated but is still an impressive sight. There is even a group working to preserve it, and talk of turning the station into a lakefront café to serve as the final destination for the Towpath Trail (see the Towpath ride), which is still to be completed at its Cleveland end.

We now set out for the ride itself, backtracking on our bikes past our vehicles and continuing on the gravel route we drove in from the shoreway. Fortunately, this portion is short and we are soon pedaling on pavement.

Factories once dotted the peninsula, and Dave tells me there is an entrance to a still-active salt mine somewhere nearby. The mine itself extends well below the city. There is still a working railroad yard on the peninsula, but it's blocked from our view by a tall hedge that runs between it and the entrance road. The area doesn't have an exclusively industrial past, however; in the nineteenth century, homes were built on the land as well. By the twentieth century, the area was used primarily by the railroads, the salt mine, and ore unloaders. There's also a marina here today. As with the Coast Guard station, plans exist to revitalize the area, this time as an entertainment district, though we don't see any signs of this as we ride through.

When we get back to the second stop sign, which is the Memorial Shoreway intersection, we cross the road and turn onto a paved trail, taking it toward the lake and into Edgewater Park. This is one of the six separate properties that make up the Cleveland Lakefront State Park system.

Reaching the lakefront, we stay on the trail as is turns southwest. We soon pass Edgewater Beach and then climb a short hill to higher ground that fronts the ongoing shoreline. From the bluffs, we look back at the eye-catching skyline. Though only a couple of the buildings qualify as skyscrapers, four or five others are sufficiently tall to give contour to the view, rising above Cleveland Browns Stadium, the Shoreway Bridge, and the many smaller structures. Looking ahead along the shoreline, we see a cluster of high-rises that Tom identifies as the "Gold Coast" area of Lakewood, which we will ride through today.

We reach a point where the trail crosses a park road, when we look to our right and see a large statue of a man standing on a pedestal. We decide to turn aside for a closer look and find, through an engraving, that the man is the German composer Richard Wagner. I later learn that German immigrants, many of whom lived in a nearby neighborhood, gave the statue to the city in 1911.

The paved trail ends at Cliff Drive, which takes us to Lake Avenue, where we continue westward. For the next few miles we stay on either Lake Avenue or Edgewater Drive, which parallels it. Edgewater is closer to the lake, but is not continuous—more like a dashed line—so where necessary, we use cross streets and drop one block south to Lake Avenue. But following Murray's dictum of generally staying as close to the lake as possible, we keep stepping back up to Edgewater in the places where it exists. The shore is full of vintage housing in a variety of classic architectural styles, and this adds a man-made beauty to accompany the natural glory of the lake.

Crossing W. 117th Street, we leave Cleveland and enter Lakewood, an inner-ring suburb. The settlement that became Lakewood was first called East Rockport, but in 1889, it incorporated as a hamlet called Lakewood. Its proximity to the lake and wealth of trees probably didn't hurt the naming process. It became a city in 1911.

Sometime before that, the Lakewood police department added bicycle patrols. The bikes were still in use in 1916, when a photo was taken showing five officers standing with their two-wheelers. The department's annual report for 1918 stated that during the preceding year, seven new bicycles had been acquired to replace old ones. By 1925, motorcycles replaced bicycles, but what goes around comes around, they say, and in the 1990s, bicycle patrols resumed. Their maneuverability makes bicycles ideal police vehicles in compact communities like Lakewood. They also make the police officers mounted on them more approachable. I contacted Lakewood's current police chief, Tim Malley, to find out about bicycle use in the department, and he told me that the department has actually increased its bicycle patrols in

Lakewood's Bike Rodeo

Police officers on bicycles aren't just about patrolling. In 2010, the Lakewood Police Department sponsored its first annual Bike Rodeo for children ages six–ten, to teach bicycle safety and skill building. Intended as a proactive way to help kids stay safe while enjoying the summer, the rodeo also helped the participants learn how to transition from riding on sidewalks (required for kids eight and under in Lakewood) to riding on the streets.

recent years. "We have all four of our neighborhood police officers on bike patrol, our part-time officers patrol on bikes, and our school resource officers patrol on bikes during non-school time," he said. And when I rode this route again in July, I saw two officers on bikes in Lakewood Park.

We come to the settlement of high-rise condos and apartment towers that Tom had previously pointed out to us as the Gold Coast, which is visible from downtown Cleveland. Like much of the shoreline property, the area once hosted the Gilded-Age mansions of families who had made their fortunes in industry, shipping, and retailing. By the 1950s, however, all of the available land in Lakewood had been developed, leaving only one direction to build—up. So thirty-five acres of land along the shore were cleared and replaced with luxury apartments and high-rise condos.

We leave the Gold Coast area, heading out onto Lake Avenue, but soon return to Edgewater. After a few blocks, Edgewater takes us straight into Lakewood Park, a shoreline green space of thirty-one acres that includes a swimming pool, tennis courts, playground, band shell, skate park, ball diamond, and Lakewood's oldest stone house, built in 1834, which is now a museum. There's also a paved trail through the park, and we roll onto it. Where it comes to the lakefront, we see a stairway heading down to the water's edge and to the Lakefront Promenade, an attractive

The Oldest Stone House Museum

Built in 1834 by settler John Honam using locally quarried sandstone, the Oldest Stone House is now operated by the Lakewood Historical Society as a window into Lakewood's past. Honam and his daughter, Isabella Hotchkiss, used the home as their family residence until 1897. The building served retail and commercial purposes for a time after that. In 1952, the Lakewood Historical Society saved the structure from the wrecking ball and moved it to its current location in Lakewood Park. Today, it is a museum of everyday life in Lakewood from 1834 to the late 1890s.

The Oldest Stone House Museum is open for guided tours on Wednesdays from 1–4 PM and Sundays from 2–5 PM. The admission is free, but donations are welcome.

brick walkway beside the water. From the top of the stairway, we look eastward and have another great view of the Cleveland skyline. At our feet is a marker, commemorating the Underground Railroad, one branch of which ended at this point, where escaped slaves boarded boats bound for Canada.

We continue through the park, eventually turning on the path between the swimming pool and the tennis courts, and following it out to Lake Avenue. A few more turns, and we enter a neighborhood called Clifton Park, an enclave of lakefront mansions that began as a summer resort in 1869, with residential subdivisions starting in 1874. It was, like Lakewood, an area for Cleveland's captains of industry and their families. Many of the first houses were summer homes, operated by servants, but they serve as year-round homes today. In 1975, the Clifton Park area was designated as a landmark because of its history and stately homes.

As we move westbound our route is interrupted by the mouth of the Rocky River, so we head south on cross streets to the Detroit–Rocky River Bridge, passing under the bridges for US20/6 and the railroad. The route is clear enough, but the street names are puzzling. The passage through Clifton Park we are riding is Lake Road, which is not Lake Avenue, which we were on earlier. Neither is it the Lake Road we will be on shortly, after we cross the Rocky River. Before we get to the river, we have to cross Clifton Boulevard, an east–west road, which should not be confused with nearby West Clifton Boulevard, which is a north–south thoroughfare. To make things more bewildering, once we cross Clifton Boulevard, our next turn is at an unsigned intersection with another east–west street called Clifton Road, but thankfully becomes Sloane Subway in the other direction. And finally, one map identifies Lake Road, which we are on, as also being named West Clifton Road. It's a cartographer's nightmare, to say nothing of how it can befuddle wandering bicyclists!

Weaving our way through all of that, we come to Detroit Avenue, which flows over the Rocky River on the bridge we are crossing. At seven hundred feet long, the Detroit–Rocky River Bridge was, at the time of its construction in 1910, the longest unreinforced concrete arch in the world.

Once across the river, we are in the city of Rocky River, named after the watercourse that forms its eastern boundary. Settlement started in there in the early 1800s, and the community incorporated as a village in 1903 and as a city in 1930.

We head north into a neighborhood of gorgeous houses, using a series of short winding streets to stay close to the lake. On the way, we pass a six-acre green space on the lakefront, Rocky River Park. It's worth the time to stop and explore it and enjoy the great view of the lake from its bluffs.

Eventually, we exit that neighborhood by following Avalon Drive out to Lake Road (US6), which, west of the Rocky River embouchure, is the path closest to the water. This takes us past another waterfront green space, Bradstreet Landing, which features a fishing pier. A short distance after Bradstreet Landing, we roll into Bay Village, which, despite its name, has actually been a city since 1950. At this point, Tom is in the lead, but he pulls over in front of a large yellow brick building. When we catch up, Tom tells us that the structure, which is now part of the Cashelmara condominium complex, was formerly Bay View Hospital. There, osteopathic surgeon Dr. Sam Sheppard practiced medicine with his father and two brothers, prior to being charged with the mur-

Bradstreet Landing

The name of this Rocky River park comes from a 1764 disaster. That summer, British Colonel John Bradstreet was leading a flotilla of sixty boats and nine canoes, bearing some fifteen hundred troops, from an encampment at Sandusky to Fort Niagara. Attempting to put into shore after dark at the low ground that is now Bradstreet Landing, the party was struck by an unexpected storm. Twenty-five boats were destroyed and others damaged. While no lives were lost in the mishap, the destruction of so many boats forced Bradstreet to send part of the group back to Fort Niagara overland. Without adequate supplies for the overland march, at least one member of the party died.

der of his wife, a case that drew nationwide attention. I remember studying this case in a political science class in college.

The building itself has a longer history than that. It was constructed in 1895 as the mansion of Washington Lawrence, one of the founders of Union Carbide Corporation, and members of his family lived in it until 1948, when it was converted into the 110-bed hospital. You can recognize the complex by the large, upright triangular stone in front bearing the name Cashelmara. The former hospital is the building to the left of the stone.

> ### Changing Gears
>
> On July 5, 1954, Marilyn Sheppard, the wife of Dr. Sam Sheppard, was murdered in their family home. Dr. Sheppard was convicted of the killing and sent to prison. His subsequent retrial in 1966 was big news in Ohio, because it revealed the prejudice and mishandling that had so flawed the initial investigation and trial. The new jury acquitted Sheppard, but the botched investigation left many wondering about his innocence.

Continuing on Lake Road, we come to our destination, the lakeside park called Huntington Reservation, part of the Cleveland Metroparks system. We turn in and proceed to the waterfront, where we can once again see the Cleveland skyline, though now more distant. Murray points us to a nearby building called the Honey Hut, which, in season, is an ice cream stand. Since we are there in early spring, we're not eating any ice cream.

After a good look around, Murray directs us to a tunnel that passes under Lake Road and takes us to more of Huntington Reservation on the south side of the highway. We remount and pedal westward through the park to Porter Creek Drive. We turn south on this street and, where it intersects with Wolf Road, we find the Lake Erie Nature & Science Center. Much of the programming and many of the interactive displays in this facility are aimed at children, to help them understand and enjoy the natural environment, but people of all ages frequent the center. It's free to the public seven days a week, and its staff also performs rehabilitation of injured wildlife.

Heading east on Wolf Road, which parallels Lake Road, we begin our return journey. We stay on Wolf to Clague Road, where we swing north to Lake Road. From that point, most of our return journey is on the same or adjacent streets as our outbound trek.

When we come to Detroit Avenue in Rocky River, however, we turn west for a couple of blocks to a restaurant on the south side of the street called Beach Cliff Tavern. They are featuring an all-you-can-eat buffet of pasta, pizza, chicken and vegetable stir-fry, and salad for $5. The food is satisfying after our journey and we certainly get our money's worth.

As we proceed with our ride and come near Edgewater Park, we are able to use Cliff Drive (which we were not on outbound) and from this vantage point we have another good view of the Cleveland skyline, a fitting denouement of this splendid ride. We then enter the trail in Edgewater Park and pedal back to Whiskey Island.

Dining in Rocky River and Gordon Square

Rocky River

Beach Cliff Tavern
19245 Detroit Road
(440) 333-4686
soups, salads, sandwiches,
wraps, and pasta

Sweet Melissa
19337 Detroit Road
(440) 333-6357
salads, sandwiches,
and wraps

Bearden's
19985 Lake Road
(440) 331-7850
Burgers, soups, and
specialty sandwiches

Danny Boy's
20251 Lake Road
(440) 333-9595
Pizza, pasta, and ribs

Gordon Square

The Big Egg
5107 Detroit Avenue
(216) 281-1600
Breakfast, salad,
and sandwiches

Gypsy Beans &
Baking Company
6425 Detroit Avenue
(216) 939-9009
European Bistro menu

Rincon Criollo
6504 Detroit Avenue
(216) 939-0992
Mexican and Caribbean

City Grill
6416 Detroit Avenue
(216) 651-2170
Pub food, breakfast,
and burgers

Stone Mad Pub
1306 W. 65th Street
(216) 281-6500
Irish food, sandwiches, and meals

Miles and Directions

0.0 Exit Wendy Park parking area, heading southwest on the entrance road

1.3 At the second stop sign, cross the road onto the trail toward Edgewater Park and Beach. Stay as close to the beach and water as you can

2.7 The trail ends at Cliff Drive. Turn left onto West Boulevard

2.8 Turn right onto Lake Avenue

3.3 Turn right onto W. 110th Street

3.4 Turn left onto Edgewater Drive

3.5 Turn right onto Harborview Drive

3.7 Turn left onto W. 115th Street

3.8 Turn right onto Edgewater Drive

4.3 Turn left onto Cove Road

4.4 Turn right onto Lake Avenue

4.8 Turn right onto Nicholson Avenue

4.9 Turn left onto Edgewater Drive

5.5 From Edgewater Drive, proceed straight into Lakewood Park. Then follow paved trail toward lake

5.7 Walkway to Lakefront Promenade. Site of Underground Railroad marker

6.0 Swimming pool. Follow path between swimming pool and tennis courts to exit park

6.1 Turn right onto Lake Avenue

6.9 Turn right onto Kenneth Lane

7.0 Turn left onto Edgewater Drive

7.4 Jog left onto Webb Road, then right onto Lake Road (not to be confused with Lake Avenue)

8.1 Cross Clifton Boulevard (US20/6 and SR2)

8.3 At unmarked intersection with Clifton Road (not to be confused with Clifton Boulevard), turn right onto Sloane Subway (goes under railroad bridge)

8.4 Turn right onto Sloane Avenue

8.6 Turn right onto Detroit Avenue and cross bridge

8.8 Turn right onto Lake Road (becomes Beach Cliff Boulevard)

9.0 Turn right onto Frazier Drive

9.6 Turn right onto Kensington Oval

9.8 Turn right onto Parkside

9.9 Turn right onto Beach Cliff Boulevard (Rocky River Park on right)

10.2 Turn right onto Avalon Drive

10.9 Turn right onto Lake Road

14.7 Turn right into Huntington Beach State Park (follow signs to Honey Hut Ice Cream)

14.9 Exit Huntington Beach through walkway tunnel under Lake Road (directly south of Honey Hut). Walkway turns right (west) on leaving tunnel; continue that direction on adjacent park road to Porter Creek Drive

15.0 Turn left onto Porter Creek Drive

15.3 Turn left onto Wolf Road

18.2 Turn left onto Clague Road

18.4 Turn right onto Lake Road

19.4 Turn left onto Avalon Drive

20.1 Turn left onto Beach Cliff Boulevard (goes under large road)

21.3 Turn left onto Detroit Avenue and cross bridge

21.4 Turn left onto Sloane Avenue and stay on Sloane as it curves to the right

21.8 Turn left on West Clifton Boulevard (not to be confused with Clifton Boulevard)

22.1 Turn right onto Clifton Boulevard

22.2 Turn left onto Webb Road

22.3 Turn right onto Lake Avenue

24.7 Turn left onto Cove Road

24.8 Turn right onto Edgewater Drive

25.9 Turn left onto Cliff Drive

26.2 Enter Lakewood Park and continue on trail, past Edgewater Beach and through Edgewater Park

27.6 Turn left on entrance road to Whiskey Island

28.9 Enter parking area near entrance gate to Coast Guard Station

To visit redeveloped Gordon Square:

0.0   On your bikes, return to Shoreway Exit on (unmarked) Island Drive. On paved path, cross exit ramp onto Father Caruso Drive under Memorial Shoreway, climb hill, and proceed through tunnel

0.2   Cross Father Caruso Drive at top of hill onto W. 65th Street, heading south

0.7   Arrive at Detroit Avenue and stop at the Gypsy Bean Coffee House on the SE corner. There are other places to dine to both the east and west. After eating, backtrack to Wendy Park

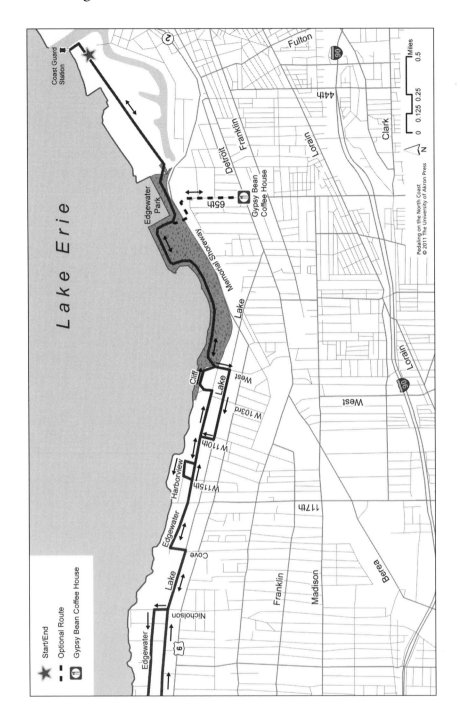

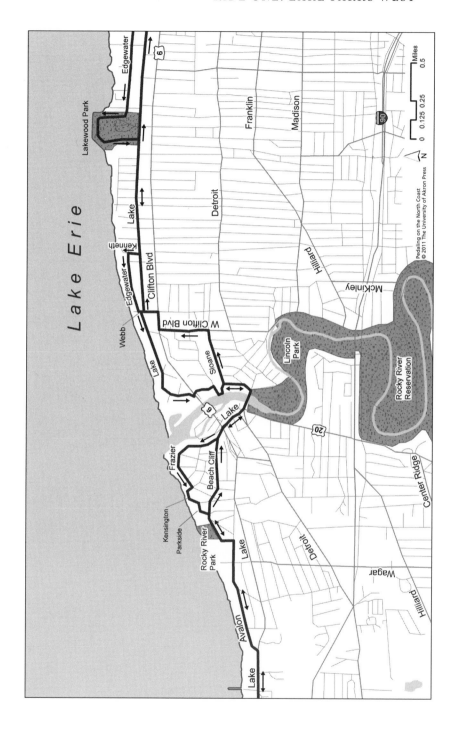

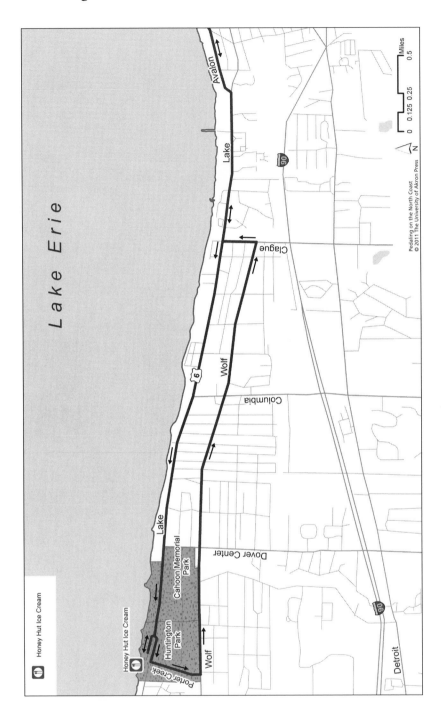

Ride 2
Cleveland Core

Route: Rockefeller Park Gardens to downtown
   Cleveland
Distance: 13 miles
Terrain: Flat
Communities Visited: Cleveland
Starting/Ending Point: Rockefeller Park Gardens, 750 E.
   88th Street, Cleveland, OH 44108
Points of Interest: Rockefeller Park Gardens, Lake Erie,
   Burke Lakefront Airport, Rock and Roll Hall of Fame,
   Great Lakes Science Center, Cleveland Browns Stadium,
   Warehouse District, Public Square, Playhouse Square,
   Euclid Corridor, Dunham Tavern Museum, Cleveland
   Clinic, Martin Luther King Jr. Boulevard
How to Get There: Take the shoreway east from Cleveland
   to the Martin Luther King Jr. Boulevard exit. Turn south on
   the MLK and then left onto E. 88th Street. Follow E. 88th as
   it bends right. Rockefeller Park Gardens is on the right side
   of the street.

Y ou have in your hands a collection of rides in the Greater Cleveland area, and, of course, the heart of Greater Cleveland is the city of Cleveland. And the "heart" of the heart, geographically at least, is Public Square and the surrounding area. This ride takes you through Public Square and past many of Cleveland's institutions and venues, including the Rock and Roll Hall of Fame, Great Lakes Science Center, Cleveland Browns Stadium, Warehouse District, Playhouse Square and more. You'll also ride along a section of Lake Erie shoreline. At just under thirteen miles, this is the shortest ride in this book, but there's so much to see that you can spend hours exploring if you wish. Additionally, the diversity of the Cleveland Core makes it ideal for re-riding.

As I'm not a Cleveland resident, I initially wondered whether riding a bike through downtown was the wisest idea. I put this question to Murray when he suggested this route. On weekdays between 9 AM and 3 PM, he said, it's not a problem. The same goes for weekends. So, avoid peak commuting times and you'll be fine.

It's a weekday in late April when Murray, Tom, Dave, and I set out to pedal the Cleveland Core. We drive to the Rockefeller Park Gardens and leave our vehicles in the lot there. These gardens are a hidden treasure in Cleveland, open daily and free to the public. While we are anxious to get started on the ride, Murray suggests I take a few moments to view the gardens. I do, and I find it time well spent. The greenhouse, filled with tropical and exotic plants, is quiet and peaceful. The outdoor gardens are colorful, filled with springtime blooms.

Mounting our bikes, we exit the lot and turn left onto E. 88th Street, which takes us down a short hill to Martin Luther King Jr. Boulevard. There, we turn toward Lake Erie, passing under I-90/Memorial Shoreway. Just after we emerge from the underpass, we turn left onto the paved, multi-purpose trail that parallels the shoreway on the north side. This takes us through Gor-

 Changing Gears

Opened in 1905, the greenhouse and outdoor gardens of Rockefeller Park Gardens were created to nurture plants for Cleveland's parks, which they still do, but eventually display gardens were added. The outdoor area features colorful seasonal and theme gardens, while the greenhouse has a water garden, tropical and exotic plants, a cactus house, a fern room, and other displays.

don Park, one of the six separate parcels in the Cleveland Lakefront State Park system. As we leave the park, the trail ends, putting us on N. Marginal Road, which is an access drive for the commercial and industrial sites between the shoreway and the lake. There's almost no traffic on it, so we pair up for conversation as we wheel on.

Beside us, cars and trucks whiz by on the shoreway, but Marginal Road is completely separate from the highway and the traffic does not intrude on our ride.

Looking at the city skyline ahead of us, I wonder if Moses Cleaveland had any idea the settlement that he platted in 1796, near the mouth of the Cuyahoga River, would become the city it is today. With its swampy lowlands and harsh winters, the settlement grew slowly at first, incorporating as the Village of Cleaveland in 1814. It became a city in 1836, but by then the spelling had been changed to "Cleveland."

We soon roll past a marina and a couple of boat clubs, reminding us why the upper side of Ohio is referred to as the nation's "North Coast."

Shortly thereafter we come to the generating plant for Cleveland Public Power, which, when it began operation in 1914, was the largest municipal light plant in the nation. It's been a political hot-point ever since, the focus of acrimonious debate over municipal ownership of utilities, but it's still in operation.

Next, we ride by the 450-acre Burke Lakefront Airport, Northeast Ohio's primary general aviation airport. Named for Thomas Burke, Cleveland's mayor at the time, the airport opened in 1948. It operates two runways but doesn't appear to be busy.

How Cleaveland Became Cleveland

According to one explanation, the spelling of the town's name changed in 1831, when the compositor at a new town newspaper, *The Cleveland Advertiser,* dropped the "a" in order to fit that moniker onto the publication's nameplate. Another account has it that the original surveyors actually misspelled the town's name when they made their first map. In any case, it appears that the "Cleveland" spelling was in use from at least 1831.

We see a few small planes and a news helicopter on the grounds, but there aren't any takeoffs or landings as we cruise by the field.

We are now near downtown and the attractions cluster close together. Just beyond Burke Airport is the *USS Cod*, a World War II era submarine open for tours and permanently docked at Cleveland's lakefront. Next to it is a U.S. Coast Guard Station.

At that point, we cross E. 9th Street. Though the road we're on continues, it becomes Erieview Road for a single block and then Alfred Lerner Drive for the next, final block.

While it's still Erieview, we cycle past the Rock and Roll Hall of Fame and Museum and the Great Lake Science Center. On the water behind it is the *William G. Mather*, a steamship built in 1925 that carried iron ore on the Great Lakes and is now a floating museum.

Next, we come to Cleveland Browns Stadium. It sits on the former site of the old Cleveland Municipal Stadium, which was the home of the Cleveland Browns football team for forty-nine years. The new stadium is the home of today's Browns.

Alfred Lerner Drive ends on W. 3rd Street, but looking straight ahead, we can see the Port of Cleveland, which includes eight international cargo docks and handles an average 12.5 mil-

Rock and Roll Hall of Fame

Rock and roll was invented in Cleveland. In the late 1940s, Leo Mintz, owner of the Record Rendezvous, noticed that young people danced around the store when rhythm and blues music was playing. But because R & B had deep southern roots and racial tones, Mintz started referring to it as rock and roll in hopes of getting it playing time on the Cleveland radio stations, which at the time, played only music from white musicians. Mintz eventually connected with Alan Freed, a disc jockey at an Akron station who began playing the R & B there. Freed moved to Cleveland radio in 1950 and the next year, with Record Rendezvous sponsoring his show, he played R & B records, but called the music rock and roll—the only DJ in the nation to do so at the time. Things grew from there.

Starting in the mid-1980s, DJ Norm N. Nite used Freed's activities to rally public support and he rallied officials to lobby to have Cleveland selected as the site for the Rock and Roll Hall of Fame. Situated on the lakefront just west of E. 9th Street, the Rock Hall opened to the public in September 1995.

lion tons of cargo per year. From our vantage point, we see only the edge of the operation. This port, along with the Rock Hall, the Science Center, the *Mather* steamship, the stadium, and the waterfront area from E. 9th Street to the mouth of the Cuyahoga River, comprise the North Coast Harbor District of Cleveland.

We turn south on W. 3rd, away from the lake and pedal downtown. We are now riding in traffic, but the streets have four lanes, and the vehicles easily scoot by us on our left. Because there are cars parked along the curb, we stay alert to make sure no one suddenly opens a car door in our path.

Changing Gears

After World War II, most of the original manufacturers and businesses left the Warehouse District, and several of the warehouses were demolished. Now the remaining warehouses have been revitalized to residences, offices, and restaurants. In 1982, the whole district was added to the National Register of Historic Places and is now one of Cleveland's premier entertainment and restaurant districts.

After two blocks, we follow Murray through a right turn and onto W. St. Clair Avenue, into the historic Warehouse District, a part of the city whose buildings once housed large hardware distributors, marine suppliers, and garment manufacturers, as well as a number of smaller wholesalers, retailers, and offices of related industries. Today, the district has been revitalized, with the remaining warehouses rehabbed into residences, restaurants, and offices. We continue through the district, turning left onto W. 9th Street. This takes us to Superior Avenue, where we turn eastward, beginning the inbound phase of the loop.

Superior leads us shortly into Public Square. This is the city's central plaza, laid out in Moses Cleaveland's original platting of the community in the 1790s. The Square occupies four city blocks, divided into quadrants by the crossing of Superior Avenue and Ontario Street. Cleveland's three tallest buildings—the Key Tower, the BP Tower, and the Terminal Tower—as well as other historic structures, surround the Square. On the Square itself sits a monument to Civil War soldiers and sailors, a statue of city founder Moses Cleaveland, and one of reformist Mayor Tom L. Johnson. In 1879, the streets of the Square became the first in the world to be illuminated by electric streetlights.

On Superior, the right-hand lane in each direction is designated for buses, which keeps it free of other traffic, so it serves as an ideal bike lane for us. We continue on Superior, riding in the canyon formed by the massive buildings on both sides of the avenue, including the Cleveland Public Library, the Federal Reserve Bank, other banks, hotels, office complexes, and the Cathedral of St. John the Evangelist, which, as the bishop's church, is the "mother parish" for over eight hundred thousand Catholics in the Diocese of Cleveland.

Coming to E. 12th Street, we turn right and wheel two blocks south to Euclid Avenue, where we turn left and enter the Theatre District, also known as Playhouse Square. It contains five renovated theatres from the 1920s and four other performance venues. The theatres present Broadway shows and other live entertainment and draw more than a million people annually.

We proceed on Euclid. On the map, the profile of this ride forms an arthritic right triangle with N. Marginal Road along the lake as the hypotenuse. That makes Euclid Avenue the longer of the two legs of the triangle. Between the 1860s and 1920s, the thoroughfare, laid out over what was once an Indian trail,

Moses Cleaveland

Moses Cleaveland, founder of the city of Cleveland, was a native of Canterbury, Connecticut, and veteran of the Revolutionary War. After his military service, he practiced law in Canterbury, and in 1788, he was a member of the Connecticut convention that ratified the U.S. Constitution. He also served several terms in the Connecticut General Assembly.

He was one of the founders and investors in the Connecticut Land Company, which purchased land in the Western Reserve in what is now Northeast Ohio. In 1796, the land company asked Cleaveland to lead a survey party to the Western Reserve to map its holdings, and he agreed, leading a group of fifty people. En route, he negotiated unhampered passage with the Native Americans living in the area. Arriving at the mouth of the Cuyahoga River on July 22, 1796, he concluded that the spot where the river met the lake and which had low banks, dense forests, and high bluffs would provide both protection and shipping access. He paced out a ten-acre New England-like public square and declared that location would serve as the capital city for the Western Reserve. His surveyors platted the town and named it Cleaveland after their leader. After completing his work, Cleaveland and most of his party returned to Connecticut, where he resumed his law practice. He never returned to Ohio.

became "Millionaire's Row," lined with the mansions of Cleveland's business and industry elite.

Later, the avenue and surrounding area fell into decline, but recently a massive urban renewal effort reclaimed the route and the adjacent neighborhoods. From a cyclist's viewpoint, the renewal makes Euclid an ideal city bike route. The city installed bus stops on islands between the opposing traffic lanes, allowing the left-hand lane in each direction to be reserved for buses. The right-hand lane is for other traffic, and between it and the curb is a narrower lane dedicated for bicycles. Additionally, with curb parking prohibited, we don't even have to worry about the possibility of being "doored" by someone opening a car door.

As we ride along Euclid Avenue in the middle of a workday, I am surprised that the traffic in the general-use lane is so light, and I comment about it to Murray. He explains that after vehicles were restricted to one lane, a lot of the through traffic moved to parallel streets, making Euclid even more bicycle-friendly.

We leave Playhouse Square and pass several Cleveland State University buildings and then pedal through an area that is a mix of retail and office space.

Crossing E. 65th Street, we come to Gallucci's Italian Foods on the right. Murray has selected Gallucci's for our lunch and says it's a "fixture" in Cleveland. While this is primarily a market, it has deli counters that serve sandwiches and hot

> **Changing Gears**
>
> Gallucci's Italian Foods
> 6610 Euclid Avenue
> (216) 881-0045
> Sandwiches and hot food

food. We all select sandwiches—Murray has the turkey, Tom the Genoa salami, Dave the ham and cheese, and I the prosciutto. After getting cold drinks from the cooler, we sit outside on picnic tables and enjoy our lunch. I saw some substantial desserts in the bakery case and, after I finish my sandwich, I go back for round two: an amazing chocolate-dipped peanut butter cookie.

Across the street and slightly east of Gallucci's is a building that appears to be an early nineteenth-century structure, which, in fact, it is. This is Dunham Tavern Museum, the oldest building in Cleveland still standing on its original site. Dating from 1824, the two-story building was the home of early settlers Rufus and Jane Pratt Dunham, but since it was situated on the Buffalo-Cleveland-Detroit post road, the Dunhams also used part of the structure as a tavern. The building is a Cleveland landmark, is listed on the Register of National Historic Places and is open to the public on Wednesday and Sunday afternoons.

Continuing our journey, we come to the campus of Cleveland Clinic, a major multispecialty medical center and teaching hospital that draws patients from all over the world. It sprawls over several blocks on both sides of Euclid Avenue. The clinic is the largest employer in Cleveland and is ranked by *U.S. News and World Reports* as the top heart hospital in America.

The cross street just beyond the clinic is E. 105th, the shorter "leg" of the right triangle. We turn left onto it and head north, toward the lake. On our right is the expansive green space of Wade Park. Its grounds boast several of Cleveland's cultural institutions, including the Cleveland Museum of Natural History, the Cleveland Botanical Gardens, the Cleveland Museum of Art, the Fine Arts Garden, and Severance Hall, a gorgeous concert space built in 1931 and the home of the Cleveland Orchestra. Also to our right, adjacent to Wade Park, is the landmark University Circle United Methodist Church, known informally as the "Church of the Holy Oil Can" due to the shape of its spire.

In quick succession, we cross Mt. Sinai Drive and Martin Luther King Jr. Boulevard. We take the next left, which is East Boulevard. It snakes along the eastern boundary of Rockefeller Park, a long, narrow, and winding green corridor with MLK Boulevard running like a backbone through it. East Boulevard parallels Martin Luther King Jr. Boulevard, but because the MLK leads directly to an exchange for the shoreway, it sustains more traffic than does East Boulevard. Although single residences and apartment buildings line the eastern side of East Boulevard, the western side is parkland.

Rockefeller Park is the home of Cleveland's Cultural Gardens, more than twenty landscaped, themed enclaves, each representing a different ethnic group within Cleveland. (According to Cleveland's Community Relations Board, more than 117 different cultures are represented in the city.) The gardens are spread out along the MLK and East Boulevard. We pass the German, Lithuanian, Greek, Slovak, Rusin (also called Carpatho-Russians), Czech, Slovenian, and Polish gardens.

Just after the last of these, we cross St. Clair Avenue at the light, and take the right fork as East Boulevard splits. This fork runs straight into E. 88th Street. We pedal another block and are back at Rockefeller Park Gardens, where we started, having seen great highlights of this city by the lake.

Miles and Directions

NOTE: *The gardens close the parking lot gates at 4 PM, so if you are going to return later than that, park instead in Gordon Park, on the west side of MLK Boulevard, just north of the shoreway overpass.*

0.0	Exit Rockefeller Park Gardens, turning left onto E. 88th Street
0.2	Turn right onto Martin Luther King Jr. Boulevard, and proceed under Memorial Shoreway
0.4	Turn left onto Lakeshore Trail, which parallels the shoreway, just south of the lake
0.7	Cross E. 72nd Street
1.7	Continue from Lakefront Trail onto N. Marginal Road (near E. 55th Street)
4.3	Cross E. 9th Street onto Erieside Avenue
4.5	Continue straight from Erieside Avenue onto Alfred Lerner Way
4.7	Turn left onto W. 3rd Street
5.0	Turn right onto W. St. Clair Avenue
5.2	Turn left onto W. 9th Street
5.3	Turn left onto W. Superior Avenue
6.1	Turn right onto E. 12th Street
6.3	Turn left onto Euclid Avenue
8.4	Gallucci's Market on right
10.0	Turn left onto E. 105th Street
10.6	Turn left onto East Boulevard
12.4	Cross E. St. Clair Avenue on East Boulevard and take the right fork to proceed onto E. 88th Street
12.6	Turn left into Rockefeller Park Gardens parking lot

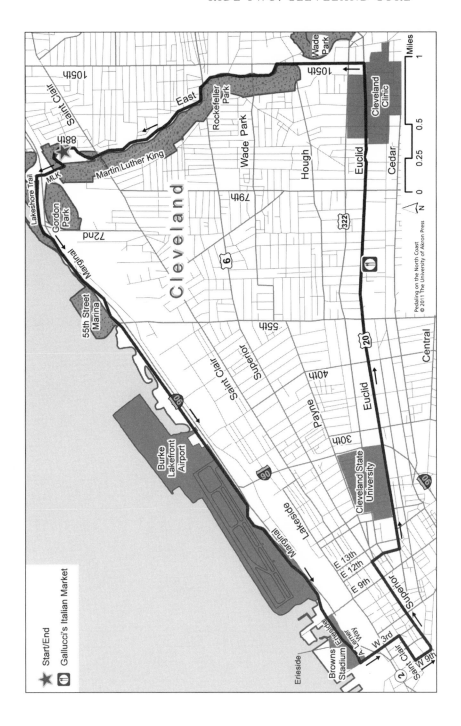

Start/End

Gallucci's Italian Market

Ride 3
Lakefront Trail East

Route: Wildwood Park to downtown Cleveland
Distance: 21 miles
Terrain: Flat
Communities Visited: Cleveland, Bratenahl
Starting/Ending Point: Wildwood Park. Enter from
Lakeshore Boulevard across from where E. 174 Street
intersects
Points of Interest: Euclid Beach, pagoda house, Bratenahl
mansions, Nike missile site, Lake Erie Shoreline, Burke
Lakefront Airport, Rock and Roll Hall of Fame, Great
Lakes Science Center, Cleveland Browns Stadium, Port of
Cleveland
How to Get There: Take the shoreway/I-90 east from
Cleveland to exit 179. Follow the exit ramp to Lakeshore
Boulevard. Turn left and follow Lakeshore Boulevard to the
entrance to the Villa Angela and Wildwood Area, on north
side of Lakeshore, across from the intersection with E. 174
Street. In the park, bear right and park in one of the lots
near the playground.

T his is a true lakefront ride, designed to explore Cleveland's lakeshore from its eastern boundary to downtown. While a portion of this route overlaps the Cleveland Core ride, this one starts farther east and sticks to the water in both directions. It also goes through the Village of Bratenahl (home to some impressive lakeside mansions), passes a former site of the Nike missile program, and cruises by Burke Lakefront Airport, the Rock and Roll Hall of Fame, the Great Lakes Science Center, Cleveland Browns Stadium and the Port of Cleveland.

The route starts near Cleveland's eastern boundary; the city of Euclid begins just a few blocks farther east. The starting point is Wildwood Park, right on the water, but don't be surprised if locals refer to it as Euclid Beach. Technically, three units of Cleveland's Lakefront State Park system cluster together there. Wildwood Park is farthest east, but Villa Angela is right next to it, and Euclid Beach is next to that, forming what appears to be a continuous waterfront park. The ride begins on a paved multi-use trail where Wildwood Park butts against Neff Road, but if you're driving to the starting point, you can't enter the park from Neff. Instead, drive in from Lakeshore Boulevard through the entrance marked "Villa Angela and Wildwood Area," across from where E. 174 Street tees into Lakeshore Boulevard.

Murray, Tom, Dave, and I pedal this route in early September, a couple of days before Labor Day weekend. We begin at the park's eastern edge at Neff Road, where the paved trail starts. A sign beside the trail identifies it as part of the Cleveland Lakefront Bikeway. This Bikeway runs seventeen miles along the lake, from Cleveland's eastern border with Euclid to its western border with Lakewood (the Lake Parks West Ride uses part of the bikeway west of downtown). The bikeway consists of both off-road trails and on-street signed routes, and this ride uses mostly bikeway.

Staying on the paved trail, we weave our way through the three parks, passing the beach on our right. Since this is a weekday, there are not a lot of swimmers, but Tom, who grew up nearby, tells us that the park will be crowded over the upcoming holiday weekend.

In less than a mile from the start, we arrive at Lakeshore Boulevard, where we turn right, heading west. Almost immediately, we pass the former site of Euclid Beach Park, once Cleveland's "Coney Island," featuring roller coasters and other rides, a fun house, picnic grounds, a dance pavilion, and a long pier extending out into the lake. It opened in 1894 and operated until 1969. All that remains of the park today is the gateway arch on Lakeshore Boulevard, which has been declared a National Historic Landmark.

A bit farther on, Lakeshore turns south for four blocks and then turns west again. At the next street, E. 151st, Tom directs us back toward the lake and to a short street along the water. One of the houses on that street resembles a single-tiered pagoda. This architecture is so unusual in Northeast Ohio that Tom felt it was worth the short detour to see it. He was right; the teal curves of the roof contrast strikingly with the Cleveland sky.

We take 149th Street to the left to rejoin Lakeshore, and continue for a few more blocks through blue-collar neighborhoods. Shortly after we pass E. 140th Street and then an exit ramp from the shoreway (both on our left), there's a change as sudden as it is dramatic. We're still on Lakeshore Boulevard, but we've crossed into the Village of Bratenahl, where the street becomes a tree-lined drive set with large estates.

Euclid Beach Park

Euclid Beach Park, encompassing ninety acres of lakefront property, was opened in 1894 by a group of Cleveland investors, and patterned after New York's Coney Island. The park was not financially successful and was sold to the Humphrey family, who had operated a popcorn stand in there. The Humphreys expanded the beach and bathing facilities and generally spruced the place up. At that time, Clevelanders could reach the location with only a single streetcar fare, so the Humphreys advertised "one fare, free gate, and no beer." The enterprise became a success, popular for family outings, business events, and community gatherings.

The park remained popular and successful into the 1960s, when rising costs, lake pollution, and other factors caused attendance to fall off. The park closed at the end of the summer in 1969. Today, the landmark archway entrance is all that remains at the site.

Bratenahl, named for one of the early families who owned land in the area, is an enclave about four miles long and less than a half-mile wide, surrounded on the east, south, and west by Cleveland and bounded on the north by Lake Erie. Incorporated as a village in 1903, it is a residential community with no commercial district. In the late nineteenth century, the picturesque area along the lake drew wealthy families from Cleveland, several of whom built large mansions along Lakeshore Boulevard. Most of those homes are still private residences today.

At the western end of Bratenahl, we come to a complex on the north side of the road that is a facility of the Defense Contract Management Command, an administrative agency for the Department of Defense. Of more interest, however, is its former life as a Nike missile base, part of a nationwide defense system dating from the Cold War era.

Just beyond the former Nike site, we bear right and enter the paved multi-use Lakefront Trail. It takes us through a green space and out to where Lakeshore Boulevard ends at the junction with Martin Luther King Jr. Boulevard. We cross the MLK and continue on the Lakefront Trail. The trail takes us through Gordon Park and past the E. 55th Street Marina, both of which are units of the Cleveland Lakefront State Park system. The trail then brings us out onto N. Marginal Road, an access drive for the commercial and industrial sites between the shoreway and the lake.

Riding now on N. Marginal, we pass a large condo building on the north side of the road called Quay 55, the first floor of which is the home of Andrea's Boardwalk Café.

Nike Missile Base

The Nike missile base, housed in Bratenahl during the Cold War, was part of a nationwide defense system. Intended to shoot down incoming bombers, the Nike Ajax missiles, stored underground, were an advance over installations that relied on artillery. Nike Hercules rockets later replaced the Ajax missiles at this site, but fortunately, none of these ever had to be activated, and later developments in weaponry eventually made them obsolete. The Bratenahl launcher area was demolished in 1973 and given over to other government uses.

Being an access road, N. Marginal has very little traffic, making it a good passageway for our ongoing ride. We pass a couple of boat clubs and the Cleveland Public Power plant and then come to Burke Lakefront Airport, a general aviation field that is also the site for the Cleveland Grand Prix auto race and the annual Cleveland National Air Show. That show, a Labor Day tradition in Cleveland, explains the current flurry of activity at Burke field as we pedal by. Even before getting to the field, however, we are treated to practice flights overhead by the Navy's famed Blue Angels F/A-18 Hornet jets. They are flying in formation and performing maneuvers, and the roar as they pass overhead punctuates our conversations throughout our ride.

> **Changing Gears**
>
> The Great Lakes Science Center, opened in 1996, is an interactive education center dedicated to "the environment, science, and technology of the Great Lakes Region." It includes hundreds of science exhibits and activities, many of them related to maritime life, as well as an Omnimax wide-screen movie theatre.

Beyond Burke Airport is the permanently docked *USS Cod*, a World War II era submarine that's open for tours. Next to it is a U.S. Coast Guard Station.

As we cross E. 9th Street, N. Marginal becomes Erieview Road briefly, and then becomes Alfred Lerner Drive for the final block. We continue, with the city skyline looming on our left. We ride past the Rock and Roll Hall of Fame and Museum and then past the Great Lake Science Center (see the Cleveland Core ride). Behind the center floats the *William G. Mather*, a 1925 steamship that carried iron ore on the Great Lakes and is now a museum. Beyond the Science Center is Cleveland Browns Stadium. Once past that, Alfred Lerner Drive ends on W. 3rd Street, and we have

---

Cleveland Browns Stadium

Cleveland Municipal Stadium was torn down following the 1996 season, after Browns owner Art Modell moved the franchise to Baltimore, where it became the Baltimore Ravens. Modell blamed his decision on the city, as they had declined to refurbish Municipal Stadium, but his move led the city to build a new stadium on the same site, which opened in July 1999. Cleveland, in a deal with the National Football League, reactivated the Browns, who occupy the new stadium.

Changing Gears

If you decide to have lunch in the warehouse district, we recommend both The Waterstreet Grill, 1265 W. 9th Street, (216) 619-1600, and Gillespie's Map Room, 1281 W. 9th Street, (216) 621-7747. Both are open seven days a week. If you are riding on Sunday, it's best to eat at one of these, as Andrea's Boardwalk Café, 5455 N. Marginal Road, (216) 432-9730, is open only Monday through Saturday.

a choice to make. Are we ready for lunch? If so, we can turn left on W. 3rd, enter downtown and within a few blocks, be at one of the restaurants in the Warehouse District. If not, we can turn right, circle the stadium, and begin the trek back toward our starting point, and stop for lunch at Andrea's Boardwalk Café. We opt for Andrea's.

Starting the circle around the stadium, we pass the entrance to the Port of Cleveland. While we can see only the nearest slice of the area, the whole port is a large operation, including eight international cargo docks and handling an average 12.5 million tons of cargo per year.

Completing our circuit of the stadium, we turn east on Erieview, cross E. 9th, and, reversing our outbound journey, have a second look at the interesting sites along the Cleveland shoreline.

When we arrive at Andrea's, we lock our bikes in the provided bike rack and head inside. The building is on a pier jutting into the lake; the upper floors are condominiums and the ground floor houses Andrea's and a parking deck. The eatery features light fare, including gourmet coffees, beverages, sandwiches, wraps, salads, and desserts. There's a choice of breads for the sandwiches, which come with a side. I go for a classic tuna salad sandwich on multigrain bread with a pickle and kettle chips.

The inside seating area has comfortable leather couches and chairs, but it's a beautiful day so we head for the tables on the outside boardwalk, which extends down the west side of the building, fronting the lake. This vantage point not only lets us view the lake while we eat, but also continue to enjoy the ongoing acrobatics of the Blue Angels.

It's tempting to linger there long after we finish eating, soaking up the sun, enjoying the sights, and feeling the breeze, but we have a few miles to go, so we remount and finish the ride.

Miles and Directions

Trail starts at Neff Road at eastern border of Wildwood Park.
Marked by a Cleveland Lakefront Bikeway sign

0.0   Head west and south from Neff Road on Lakefront Trail

0.2   Turn left with trail (over white bridge) on Villa Angela Drive

0.2   Turn right onto trail immediately after crossing bridge

0.5   Turn left with trail (away from lake)

0.8   Turn right onto Lakeshore Boulevard

1.6   Turn right onto E. 151st Street

1.8   Turn left onto Shore Acres Drive (look for the pagoda house)

1.9   Turn left onto E. 149th Street

2.1   Turn right onto Lakeshore Boulevard

5.7   Bear right to leave Lakeshore Boulevard and enter Lakefront Trail

6.1   Turn right at Martin Luther King Jr. Boulevard to continue on Lakefront Trail

6.4   Cross E. 72nd Street

7.0   Cross N. Marginal Road at park entrance, continue on Lakefront Trail

7.4   Continue from Lakefront Trail onto N. Marginal Road

7.5   Boardwalk Café at Quay 55

10.0   Cross E. 9th Street onto Erieside Avenue

10.2   Continue straight from Erieside Avenue onto Alfred Lerner Way

10.4   Turn right on W. 3rd Street and circle Cleveland Browns Stadium

10.9   When you arrive back at Alfred Lerner Way, turn left onto Erieside, and follow route in reverse back to starting point

21.1   Arrive at Wildwood Park parking area

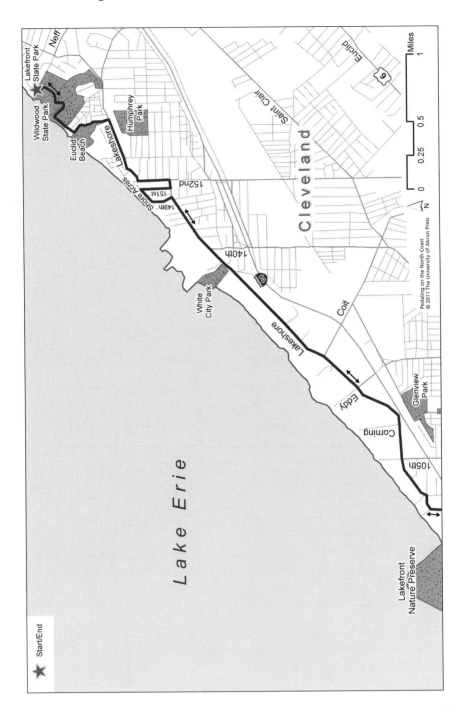

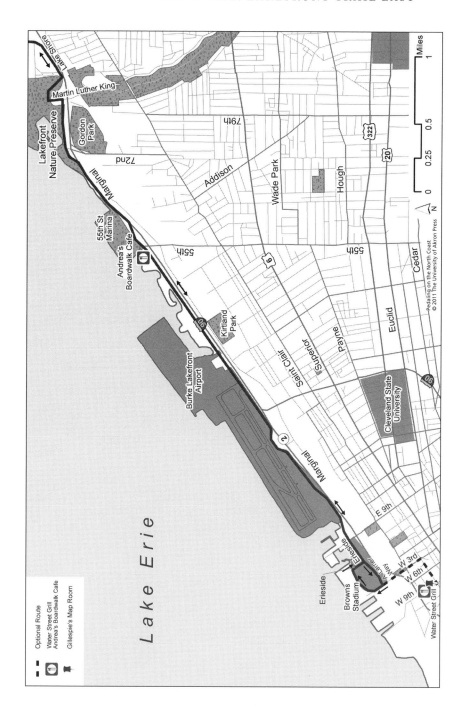

Optional Route
Water Street Grill
Andrea's Boardwalk Cafe

Gillespie's Map Room

Lake Erie

Lakefront Nature Preserve

Martin Luther King

Gordon Park

Lake Shore

Marginal

55th St Marina

Andrea's Boardwalk Cafe

79th

72nd

Addison

Wade Park

Hough

322

20

55th

55th

6

Cedar

Kirtland Park

Burke Lakefront Airport

Saint Clair

Superior

Payne

Euclid

90

Cleveland State University

2

Marginal

E 9th

Erieside

Browns Stadium

Erieside

Mariner

W 3rd

W 6th

W 9th

Water Street Grill

Lake Erie

Pedaling on the North Coast
© 2011 The University of Akron Press

N

0   0.25   0.5   1
Miles

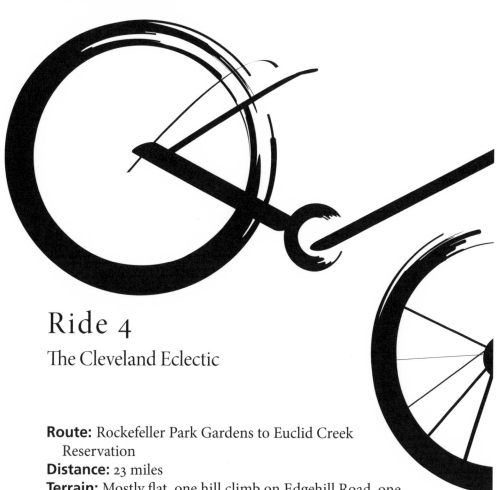

Ride 4
The Cleveland Eclectic

Route: Rockefeller Park Gardens to Euclid Creek
Reservation

Distance: 23 miles

Terrain: Mostly flat, one hill climb on Edgehill Road, one
downhill in Euclid Creek Reservation

Communities Visited: Cleveland, Cleveland Heights, South
Euclid, Euclid, Bratenahl

Starting/Ending Point: Gordon Park lakefront parking
lot, just west of the MLK Boulevard intersection with
Lakeshore Boulevard

Points of Interest: Cultural Gardens, Cleveland Botanical
Garden, Cleveland Art Museum, Cleveland Museum of
Natural History, Case Western Reserve University, Little
Italy, Euclid Creek Reservation, Lake Erie, Bratenahl

How to Get There: Take the shoreway east from Cleveland
to the Martin Luther King Jr. Boulevard exit. Gordon
Park lakefront parking lot is next to the MLK Boulevard
intersection with Lakeshore Boulevard, on the west side of
the MLK and north of the shoreway.

W e built this route to close a gap. As Murray and I selected rides for this book, we drew each one on the same master map to get an overview of how they spread across the Greater Cleveland area. We intentionally avoided a couple of areas where the traffic patterns weren't conducive to bicycling, but even after allowing for those, we noticed a gap between Rockefeller Park and Euclid Creek Reservation. We made this circuit to connect them.

Murray, Tom, and Dave have all ridden through that area, but hadn't tried to make that specific park-to-reservation connection. So we turned to a Clevelander who does most of his traveling on two wheels, Marty Cooperman. Marty loves the outdoors and sees no reason to drive a car when a bicycle will do, even in deep winter. Consequently, he is constantly on the lookout for bike-friendly routes through urban areas. Marty, Tom, Dave, and Murray pooled their knowledge of Cleveland and the northeast 'burbs and came up with this wide-roving route that includes a major cultural area, unique neighborhoods, parklands, and lakefront. This ride has more turns than most others in this book, but the route is not difficult to follow, and we suspect that once you learn it, you'll want to ride it again.

On a hot day in late August, Murray, Wayne, Dave, Tom, and I start this ride from the lakefront parking lot at Gordon Park. While we did not consult with one another beforehand, it turns out that four of us are mounted on Treks: Dave on an 1100 road bike, Tom on an Antelope 830 mountain bike, Wayne on a Pilot racing bike, and I'm on my 520 touring bike. Murray, the Trekless one of the bunch, is riding his trusty Bruce Gordon BLT.

Leaving the lot, we turn south onto the paved multi-use Harrison Dillard Trail and pass under the shoreway. The trail runs through Rockefeller Park, paralleling Martin Luther King Jr. Boulevard on its west side. Actually, there is trail on both sides of the road, but Murray tells us that the one on the east ends before the road does. What's more, by using the west path, we don't have to cross the MLK, which is a good thing, because it is a busy roadway.

Rockefeller Park is a slender natural preserve along the northern stretch of Doan Brook. An oasis in the midst of the city, the park was created from a 276-acre gift to Cleveland from industrialist John D. Rockefeller in 1897. The MLK Boulevard, a winding parkway through the preserve, sustains a lot of traffic, but the parklands on each side of the road are quiet and pleasant. As we ride from north to south down the length of the park, we see the brook, woods, fields, fountains, a playground, and a few of Cleveland's Cultural Gardens. These are landscaped, themed enclaves, each representing a different ethnic group within Cleveland. Within the whole park, there are currently more than twenty of them, with additional ones planned, but not all front on the MLK. (We visited other cultural gardens on East Boulevard on the Cleveland Core ride.)

Arriving at E. 105th Street, we are at the end of the park, but the MLK Boulevard continues. We cross 105th with other vehicles at the signal light, proceed to the right, part way around a traffic circle, and pedal a short distance farther on the MLK. Then a quick left on Jeptha Drive takes us up a short hill to Wade Park Oval. This circular drive hosts the Cleveland Museum of Natural History, which is to our left, and the Cleveland Museum of Art, which we pass as we continue on our route, as well as the Cleveland Botanical Garden, which we also pass. A series of quick turns then takes us through part of the campus of Case Western Reserve University and eventually out to Euclid Ave-

Cleveland Museum of Natural History

Preceded by three previous Cleveland institutions that focused on natural history, the Cleveland Museum of Natural History was launched in 1920. All of these closed by the end of the nineteenth century, but the CMNH inherited some of the previous collections. The museum's present facility was built between 1958 and 1961 and has been expanded since. The collection includes more that one million specimens in eleven disciplines, with such notables as "Lucy," a hominid who, at the time of her discovery, was the earliest known link in the chain of human evolution, dinosaurs, and the giant Cleveland Shale fish. The museum also features a planetarium, an observatory, and live animal shows.

nue. The area including Wade Park and Case Western Reserve is known as University Circle.

We turn left on Euclid and follow it as it goes under a bridge carrying tracks of the Regional Transit Authority. Immediately after the bridge, we turn right onto Coltman Road and then right again onto E. 119th Street. On our right are RTA tracks and, as we pass, we spot an RTA train traveling along them.

E. 119th ends on Mayfield Road, were we turn left. As we do, we enter Little Italy, a fact that's noted on a roadside sign and also by a mural painted on a retaining wall on the south side of Mayfield. The mural includes the words in Italian, *La Storia del Popolo Italo-Americano*—"The history of the Italian-American people."

Little Italy features art galleries, shops, and several popular Italian restaurants. As we turn off of Mayfield onto Random Road, Murray points up Mayfield and tells me that Presti Bakery and Mama Santa Restaurant, a couple of his favorites, are one block farther east. A couple of turns later, Murray points to a building that once housed a restaurant called Theresa's, and tells us that he took his very first date there.

This neighborhood is also the site of some food "firsts." In 1906, Angelo Vitantonio, a resident of Little Italy, invented the first pasta machine. After receiving a patent, he established a company in the neighborhood to make the machines. Another neighborhood resident who became even more well known was Ettore Boiardi—Chef Boy-ar-dee,—who opened his first restaurant in Little Italy in the 1940s and went on to develop the now-famous line of pasta products sold worldwide. Cleveland's Little

Cleveland Museum of Art

Considered among the finest art museums in the U.S., the Cleveland Museum of Art is in possession of a comprehensive collection of renowned art. Opened in 1916, the neoclassical building housing the museum was constructed of white Georgian marble. In the years since, the museum has expanded four times, with most recent expansion expected to be completed in 2013. Although the museum charges for admission to special exhibitions, admission to the permanent collection is free.

Italy also has a historical claim to notoriety for once being home to a branch of the Mafia.

Our path takes us across Murray Hill Road, which is the heart of Little Italy, onto Edgehill Road, where we pedal uphill into Cleveland Heights (where we'll return in The Heights ride). At the top of the hill, we cross Overlook Road to continue on Edgehill. This neighborhood has large, older well-kept homes on shady streets. Dave mentions his familiarity with this area; before he married, he had lived in an apartment building just a block away.

We proceed for several blocks on Edgehill and then turn right onto Washington Boulevard, another tree-lined street, to continue eastward. The houses on this street aren't quite as large as the section we just left, but they are just as well-kept.

We stay on Washington as we cross Lee Road, where Cleveland Heights High School sits on the southeast corner. Murray mentions that he graduated from there, Class of 1957.

Washington Boulevard breaks off at S. Taylor Road and then resumes a block farther east. We loop around on a side street to reach the second section of Washington. As we reach it, we enter University Heights momentarily (also explored in The Heights ride), a community so named because the campus of John Carroll University is within its boundaries. Our next turn takes us back into Cleveland Heights.

We are now moving northward, working our way through a series of neighborhood streets. Eventually, we cross Mayfield Road, which Murray says is the northern end of an Orthodox Jewish neighborhood. The next area is still residential, and after

Cleveland Botanical Garden

Established in 1930 as the Garden Center of Cleveland, this is the nation's oldest civic garden center. Its mission is "to spark a passion for plants and cultivate an understanding of their vital relationship to people and the environment." Some of that is accomplished through its plant science curriculum, used with more than 12,500 children annually, but the garden is also a significant informational and inspirational resource for backyard gardeners. The institution has twenty specialty gardens and indoor biotic communities.

a few blocks, we turn eastward again, now on Elmwood Road. After a couple of blocks, we enter South Euclid.

In 1797, Moses Cleaveland, the founder of Cleveland, named the area east of the Cuyahoga River Euclid, after the Greek mathematician and patron saint of surveyors. That area became Euclid Township in 1809 and was later divided into nine districts, with South Euclid one of them. In the 1850s, a portion of South Euclid became the village of Bluestone, named for the blue-gray siltstone quarried along Euclid Creek. That village no longer exists, but one of the South Euclid streets is named Bluestone. South Euclid became a village in 1917 and a city in 1941.

Eventually, we are on another eastbound street called W. Anderson, which brings us out to S. Green Road, one of the busier thoroughfares in the area. Somewhat confusingly, S. Green splits briefly into two roadways at this particular point, W. Green and E. Green respectively, and branches around a block of land that includes a small triangular park, the site of the South Euclid War Memorial. Because W. Green is busy and there is no traffic signal, we dismount and walk the bikes across the street to the

Case Western Reserve University

Case Western Reserve University, the largest private university in Ohio, fills one hundred and fifty acres in University Circle and offers both undergraduate and graduate degrees. The school grew out of a college founded by David Hudson in 1826, in Hudson, Ohio (see the Aurora Farm and Western Reserve Ramble rides). The school, named Western Reserve College, was modeled on Yale University and had several Yale graduates on its staff. Not surprisingly, it was sometimes called "the Yale of the West."

In 1880, philanthropist Leonard Case Jr. gave one million dollars to establish the Case School of Applied Science in Cleveland. By that time, Cleveland had emerged as the major population center of the region, and so in 1882, when another donor provided over five hundred thousand dollars to move Western Reserve College to Cleveland, the school did so, renamed as Western Reserve University. Other donors made possible a land purchase that enabled both schools to share side-by-side campuses. WRU developed liberal arts and professional programs, while Case became a strong school of science and engineering. There were discussions of merger as early as 1890, but the two institutions did not formally merge until 1967.

park. We jog left on the sidewalk to E. Green, below the park, where we remount and follow E. Green behind the park to the entrance to Euclid Creek Reservation.

This reservation is one of the Cleveland Metroparks, but is not connected at its borders to other parks in the system the way those in the "Emerald Necklace" are. Nonetheless, Euclid Creek is a great addition to the park system. It's a wide corridor park on both sides of Euclid Creek, which runs the length of the reservation. As soon as we enter, we are met with a pleasant, verdant environment. While, as in Rockefeller Park, there is a road lengthwise through this park, this one bears far less traffic than MLK Boulevard. We enter the paved multi-use trail beside the road. At first, the trail is on the west side of the park road. A short way into the park it crosses to the east side of the road, putting us right beside Euclid Creek as it streams past cliffs of shale. In terms of views of the waterway, the trail is superior to the road.

Our other pleasant discovery is that our whole passage through the park is downhill. Just as the creek flows toward Lake Erie, so do we, and we pedal easily to keep moving.

Less than halfway through the park, we cross an unmarked boundary and enter the city of Euclid. Like South Euclid, Euclid was originally part of Euclid Township. It became a village in 1903 and a city in 1930.

Euclid Creek Reservation has six separate picnic areas along its length and lots of space for walking, cycling, meditating, and simply enjoying nature, but soon we come to its north end, where we turn left onto Highland Road and run northwest toward the lake. Though we have now lost sight of Euclid Creek, a later look at the map shows that it continues toward Lake Erie, not far east of Highland.

As we proceed, Highland becomes Dille Road, named for the family of David Dille, a lieutenant from the Revolutionary War who is considered the founder of Euclid Township. It isn't Dille for long, though, because at the point where we cross a double set of railroad tracks, leaving Euclid and re-entering Cleveland, the road name changes to Nottingham. A bit farther on, at a bend to the left, it becomes E. 185th Street and heads straight north. While it is still Dille/Nottingham, it passes through an area of mixed commercial and industrial use, but after it becomes E. 185th, it is primarily commercial and retail.

We are now in the area where Tom grew up. He tells us that the surrounding neighborhood once was largely populated by people of Lithuanian, Slovenian, and Croatian descent and points out a building that once housed his favorite bar, called The Two Cros. It's pronounced "crows," but these Cros weren't birds, but the two Croatian men who owned it.

It is on E. 185th that we have lunch. We pick the branch of a local coffee house chain, Arabica. Its fare includes sandwiches and wraps, and each of us has one or the other. Afterward, Murray and I return to the counter and purchase fresh-baked cookies.

Back on the bikes, we continue on E. 185th to its intersection with Lakeshore Boulevard, which is the closest continuous road to the lake between the eastern boundary of Cleveland and Rockefeller Park. We turn west on Lakeshore, in front of Villa Angela St. Joseph High School. Lakeshore is lined with homes, and we take it several blocks to Shenely Avenue, where we turn right. This short street takes us directly to the lakefront, where we turn left on a short street along the shore. We follow this for three blocks and enter Wildwood Park.

Wildwood is one of three units of Cleveland's Lakefront State Park system that sit side by side at water's edge. The other two are Villa Angela and Euclid Beach, but for all practical purposes, the three recreational units form one continuous water-

Dining Options on E. 185th Street

Gus's Diner 185
797 E. 185th Street
(216) 481-8781
Salads, sandwiches,
and signature burgers

Arabica Coffee House
818 E. 185th Street
(216) 486-7777
Sandwiches, salads,
wraps, coffees, pastries

Muldoon Saloon and Eatery
1020 E. 185th Street
(216) 531-3130
Dinners, sandwiches, pizza

front park. We roll into the park on an entrance road that has five poles staked across its mouth to prevent cars from using it, but allowing pedestrians and cyclists easy entrance. We then wind through a parking lot, and wheel onto the paved Cleveland Lakefront Bikeway. We follow this to and across a white bridge that spans a watercourse. This is Euclid Creek again, completing its run to Lake Erie. Looking to our right from the bridge, we see the mouth of the creek, joining the lake.

Across the bridge, we turn right to continue on the trail, and roll past Euclid Beach on our left. The weather is warm, but on this weekday, there aren't many swimmers in the water. Tom, who grew up in the area, says that it is a beautiful beach and, in his opinion, it's underused.

A bit farther on, the trail turns left toward Lakeshore Boulevard, but Tom knows a way to keep us by the water a little longer. We follow him through the paved beachfront seating area of the park and then roll into the adjacent parking lot of two multistory apartment buildings. Beyond the second one, we encounter a metal fence that ends our progress along the lakefront, but we wheel beside it away from the lake to a pedestrian exit, which we roll through onto E. 156th Street. This returns us to Lakeshore Boulevard, where we turn right and continue our westbound journey.

Eventually, we roll into Bratenahl and notice a significant change. The village is an enclave about four miles long and less than a half-mile wide, surrounded on the east, south, and west by Cleveland and bounded on the north by Lake Erie. It has no commercial district, but includes several substantial residences: large mansions built in the late nineteenth century and situated on large tracts of carefully landscaped waterfront land. Most are still occupied today. Through Bratenahl, Lakeshore is a tree-lined street and we enjoy the passage while checking out the unique homes.

At the western end of Bratenahl, we bear right off of Lakeshore and enter the paved multi-use Lakefront Trail that takes us through Gordon Park, to where Lakeshore Boulevard ends at the junction with Martin Luther King Jr. Boulevard. We turn right into the parking area, completing the Cleveland Eclectic circuit.

Miles and Directions

The ride begins and ends at Gordon Park lakefront parking lot, just west of the Martin Luther King Jr. Boulevard intersection with Lakeshore Boulevard.

0.0   Depart Gordon Park lakefront parking lot, turning left onto Lakefront trail. Turn right onto Harrison Dillard Trail, on the right side of MLK Boulevard, heading south. Pass under the shoreway

2.3   Follow MLK Traffic Circle at 105th Street around to right, to continue on MLK Boulevard

2.4   Turn left onto Jeptha Drive

2.5   Turn right onto Wade Oval Drive

2.7   Turn left onto East Boulevard

2.8   Turn right onto Juniper Road

2.8   Turn right onto Ford Drive

2.9   Turn left onto Bellflower Road

3.1   Turn right onto E. 115th Street

3.2   Turn left onto Euclid Avenue. Continue under railroad bridge tracks

3.4   Turn right onto Coltman Road and then an immediate right onto E. 119th Street

3.7   Turn left onto Mayfield Road. CAUTION getting out onto Mayfield

3.8   Turn right onto Random Road (Presti Bakery and Mama Santa Restaurant are one block east on Mayfield)

4.1   Turn left onto Cornell Road

4.1   Cross Murray Hill Road and continue straight onto Edgehill Road

4.4   Cross Overlook Road and bear right to continue on Edgehill Road

4.9   Cross Euclid Heights Boulevard and continue on Edgehill Road

5.3   Cross Coventry Road and continue on Edgehill Road

5.4   Turn right onto Washington Boulevard

6.1   Cross Lee Road

6.6   Turn left onto Hampstead Road

6.7   Turn right onto Superior Road

6.8	Cross S. Taylor Road
6.9	Turn left onto Washington Boulevard
7.0	Turn left onto Thayne Road
7.2	Turn right onto Cummings Road
7.4	Turn left onto Staunton Road
7.7	Turn right onto Bainbridge Road
7.8	Turn left onto Maple Road
8.1	Turn left onto S. Wood Road. Follow S. Wood as it bears right and becomes Crest Road
8.7	Jog left onto Mayfield Road and then right onto Cleveland Heights Boulevard. CAUTION: Mayfield is a busy road. Use traffic signal and walk bikes across road
8.9	Turn left with Cleveland Heights Boulevard
9.2	Turn right with Summit Park Road
9.4	Jog left onto Noble Road and then right onto Elmwood Road
10.0	Cross S. Belvoir Boulevard
10.2	Turn left onto Homestead Road
10.5	Turn right onto W. Anderson Road
10.8	Jog right on W. Green Road, around park with monument, and then left on Anderson/E. Green Road
10.9	Turn left onto E. Green Road
11.0	Turn right onto Euclid Park Road/Metropolitan Park Boulevard
13.5	Turn left onto Highland Road
13.9	Cross Euclid Avenue/US6/20. Highland becomes Dille Road. Dille Road becomes Nottingham Road
14.6	Cross St. Clair Avenue
14.8	Bear right with roadway onto E. 185th Street
15.4	Arabica Café on left
16.2	Turn left onto Lakeshore Boulevard
16.7	Turn right onto Schenely Avenue
17.0	Turn left onto Dorchester Drive
17.1	Bear right onto E. Park Drive
17.2	Cross Neff Road and enter Wildwood Park
17.3	Turn left through second parking lot

17.4   Turn right onto Lakefront Trail

17.5   Turn left over white bridge on Villa Angela Drive

17.6   Turn right onto Lakefront Trail immediately after crossing bridge

17. 9   When trail turns left away from lakefront, continue along lakefront through park, and then behind two white and blue apartment building, using paved path and parking. Proceed left around second apartment building

18.2   Turn right through pedestrian gate to exit apartment building parking lot, and then turn left onto E. 156th Street

18.3   Turn right onto Lakeshore Boulevard

22.6   Bear right to leave Lakeshore Boulevard and enter Lakefront Trail

23.0   Turn right with trail on west side of Martin Luther King Jr. Boulevard interchange with Lakeshore Boulevard and enter Gordon Parking lakefront parking lot

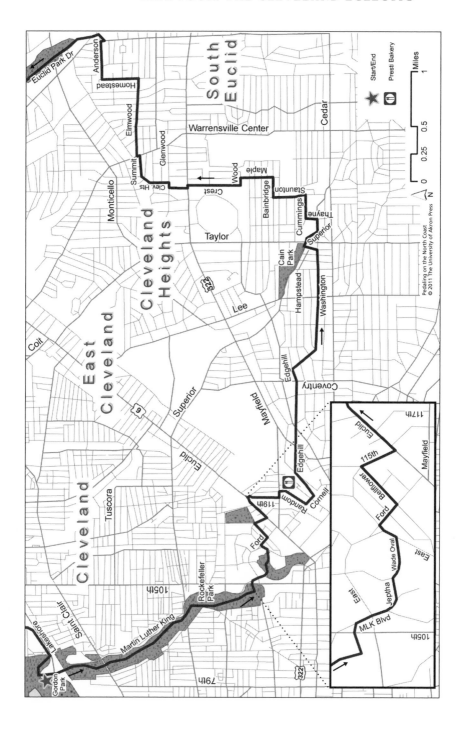

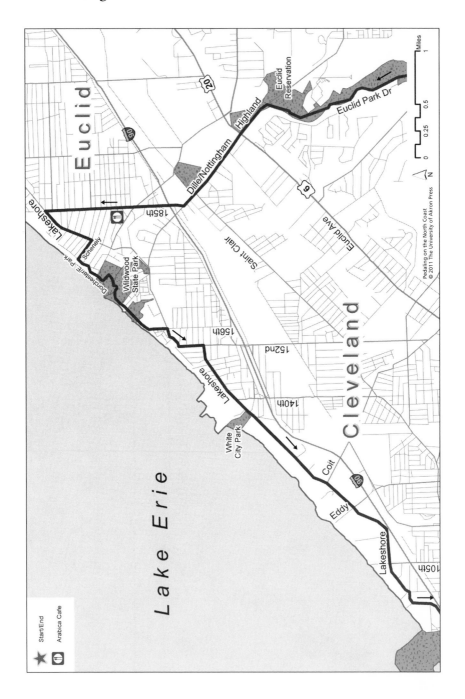

Ride 5
The Zoo Ride

Route: Leonard Krieger CanalWay Center to
   Cleveland Metroparks Zoo
Distance: 11 miles
Terrain: Mostly flat, one hill outbound and two inbound
Communities Visited: Cuyahoga Heights, Cleveland
Starting/Ending Point: Leonard Krieger CanalWay Center,
   Cleveland Metroparks, 4524 E. 49th Street, Cleveland, Ohio
   44125
Points of Interest: Leonard Krieger CanalWay Center,
   Towpath Trail, Ohio & Erie Canal, Treadway Creek Trail,
   Cleveland Metroparks Zoo
How to Get There: Take I-77 to the Harvard Road exit. Go
   west on Harvard Road to E. 49th Street. Turn left (south)
   on E. 49th and proceed to the entrance road to the Leonard
   Krieger CanalWay Center, which will be on the right side of
   the road.

H ere's a ride that's perfect for the whole family. Not only do both ends of the ride offer attractions of interest to kids and grown-ups alike—the Cleveland Zoo and the CanalWay Center—but the journey itself is relatively easy and does not put riders in competition with much traffic. At around eleven miles, the ride is reasonable for many. Additionally, there is the option of riding one way to the zoo, turning the ride into a little over five miles. Just make sure you have return transportation arranged for you and the bikes.

Outbound, there is one hill to climb, which is a consideration when riding with children, but it is on a paved trail through a wooded setting and this makes walking the hill easy and safe. The return trip involves two climbs: one right after exiting the zoo, and one up to the CanalWay Center at the end, and both of these are also on trails.

The Leonard Krieger CanalWay Center is more than just a convenient place to begin this ride. The center is comprised of an exhibit room with interpretive displays on people, nature, and industry in the Cuyahoga Valley along with a gift shop, art, and several hands-on activities for kids.

Murray, Tom, and I set out on a sunny day in early April. Murray is on his Bruce Gordon BLT, Tom on his Surly Cross-Check, and I am on my Specialized Sequoia. All of the surfaces on this route are paved, including those on trail.

The CanalWay Center is located within the village of Cuyahoga Heights, which was formerly part of nearby Newburgh Heights. It parted company with Newburgh Heights in 1918 over tax expenditures and became its own village. It has since become home to numerous industries and businesses.

All three of us have visited the CanalWay Center before, so we aim our bikes at the entrance of the multi-use trail and roll downhill through woodlands awaking after the winter hiatus. This trail soon delivers us to the paved Towpath Trail, where we turn north and wheel along beside remnants of the old Ohio & Erie Canal. In this area, the Towpath Trail corridor is flanked on both sides by industrial sites, many no longer active. Yet, thanks to the preservation work of the Cleveland Metroparks, the main impression we have from the trail is of riding through a green oasis, not through an industrial desert. Along the path, there are many informative signs on nature and history. Combined with the primer at CanalWay, these signs provide an educational backdrop to a great ride. We stop at a trailside display of steel products once made nearby and gain an idea of how much history is here.

The Towpath Trail ends at W. Harvard Avenue. Although Harvard is a busy road farther east, it is fairly tame here at its western extremity. It is easy to pedal it with children. We turn left on Harvard and ride the short distance to Jennings Road, where we turn left again. Jennings has a paved shoulder, so though there is a little more traffic on this road, our passage is easy.

At Crestline Avenue, we turn right and cruise under the bridge bearing the Jennings Freeway. Right after we emerge from the underpass, we turn left onto Treadway Creek Trail, which immediately takes us into a vibrant, green ravine that is home to the burbling Treadway Creek. As we pump upward beside the stream, the trees and other plant life around us so block our view of nearby neighborhoods that we could have been in deep woods. Along the trail, we see interpretive signboards and occasional park benches.

At the top, the trail ends in Harmody Park, a small neighborhood recreational area. We exit the park onto Plymouth Road and then, following Tom's lead, we weave through a series of quiet, residential streets. Because there is no single bike-friendly thoroughfare, we make numerous turns using one street after another for a block or two each, and the effort moves us continuously northwestward until we finally emerge on Henninger Road to Pearl Road/W. 25th Street.

Unlike the neighborhood streets, Pearl is a busy road. Though we have to travel only a block to our right, we walk our bikes on the sidewalk until we reach Wildlife Way. At the intersection with Wildlife Way, we also walk our bikes across Pearl Road when the traffic light is in our favor. Then, again waiting for the traffic signal, we cross the mouth of Wildlife Way. Once on the north side of Wildlife way, we remount and start rolling down the sidewalk, which, after a short distance, becomes a multi-use trail that takes us down the hill and to the zoo entrance road.

Although we don't plan on touring the zoo today, we turn in and follow the road to the ticket plaza. There, a park employee points out bicycle racks near the ticket plaza. (Be sure to bring along enough locks to secure all of your bikes to the racks.)

The Cleveland Zoo has some three thousand animals representing more than six hundred species, including the largest collection of primate species in North America. In addition to several outdoor settings, ranging from African Savannah to Wallaby Walkabout, the zoo also has a renowned RainForest in an enclosed building. The RainForest features over six thousand plants and six hundred animals in the largest indoor exhibit of its kind in the United States. The zoo is open to the public every day of the year, except January 1 and December 25. It also has a food court for dining during your visit.

For our return journey, we climb back up Wildlife Way, retrace our route back across Pearl Road and back down the sidewalk to Henninger Road, where we turn left. A few strokes of the pedal down Henninger, we see a sign telling us that Henninger becomes one way ahead, meaning that we are about to go the wrong way on a one-way street. However, Tom, who lives in the area, tells us to disregard the sign and proceed. He does it often on a bicycle, he says. He explains that the sign is to keep commuters from cutting through the neighborhood during rush hour. We saw no traffic on Henninger on our outbound ride and see none on it now, so we continue without incident.

The rest of our ride is a retrace in reverse of our outbound journey, and it's every bit as enjoyable as the ride in.

The Cleveland Zoo and RainForest

The Cleveland Metroparks Zoo and the RainForest are open year-round from 10 AM–5 PM, except January 1 and December 25.

On Saturdays, Sundays, and holidays from Memorial Day through Labor Day, both facilities remain open until 7 PM

Admission charges are reasonable. On Mondays, admission is free to the Zoo, but not the RainForest, for residents of Cuyahoga County and Hinckley Township. Members of reciprocal zoos receive free or discounted admission to the Zoo and the RainForest for everyone listed on the membership card.

Miles and Directions

Start at the Leonard Krieger CanalWay Center, Cleveland Metroparks, 4524 E. 49th Street, Cleveland, Ohio 44125.

0.0	Leave the center, heading west down the hill to the Towpath Trail. Cross the bridge
0.4	Turn right onto the Towpath Trail. Trail ends at W. Harvard Avenue
2.7	Turn left onto W. Harvard Avenue
2.9	Turn left onto Jennings Road
3.0	Turn right onto Crestline Avenue, go under bridge and then turn left onto Treadway Creek Trail
3.6	At end of trail, bear right at kiosk and turn right onto Plymouth Road
3.7	Turn right onto Mayview Avenue
3.8	Turn right onto W. 19th Street
3.8	Turn left onto Creston Avenue
3.9	Jog left onto Valley Road, then right onto W. 20th Street
4.1	Turn left onto Fergus Avenue
4.2	Turn left onto W. 21st Street
4.2	Turn right onto Boyer Avenue
4.3	Turn right onto W. 23rd Street
4.4	Turn left onto Henninger Road
4.6	Turn right onto Pearl Road/W. 25th Street. STAY ON SIDEWALK to traffic light
4.7	WALK BIKE AND CROSS PEARL ROAD AT INTERSECTION to Wildlife Way. Then cross Wildlife Way and turn left on Wildlife Way. Use sidewalk, which becomes multi-use trail
5.0	Turn right into zoo entrance road. Follow signs to ticket plaza
5.3	Ticket plaza and bicycle parking (we recommend you bring a bike lock and chain to secure your bikes while you visit the zoo)
5.3	Backtrack out of zoo and up Wildlife Way to Pearl Road/W. 25th Street

5.8 Cross Wildlife Way and then Pearl Road, walking bike at intersection. Turn right on Pearl Road, but stay on sidewalk on left

5.9 Turn left onto Henninger Road. After about a block, Henninger is marked one way, coming toward you. Disregard one-way sign and proceed on Henninger (traffic is light on this short street, and you will not be going the wrong way long)

6.2 Turn left onto W. 23rd Street

6.2 Turn left onto Boyer Avenue

6.3 Turn left onto W. 21st Street

6.4 Turn right onto Fergus Avenue

6.4 Turn right onto W. 20th Street

6.6 Jog left onto Valley Road, then right onto Creston Avenue

6.7 Turn right onto W. 19th Street

6.8 Turn left onto Mayview Avenue

6.9 Turn left onto Plymouth Road

7.0 Turn left into park and enter Treadway Creek Trail

7.5 Turn right onto Crestline Avenue

7.6 Turn left onto Jennings Road

7.8 Turn right onto W. Harvard Road

8.0 Turn right into Towpath Trail parking lot and enter Towpath Trail

10.3 Turn left onto bridge and side trail up to CanalWay Center

10.7 Arrive at CanalWay Center

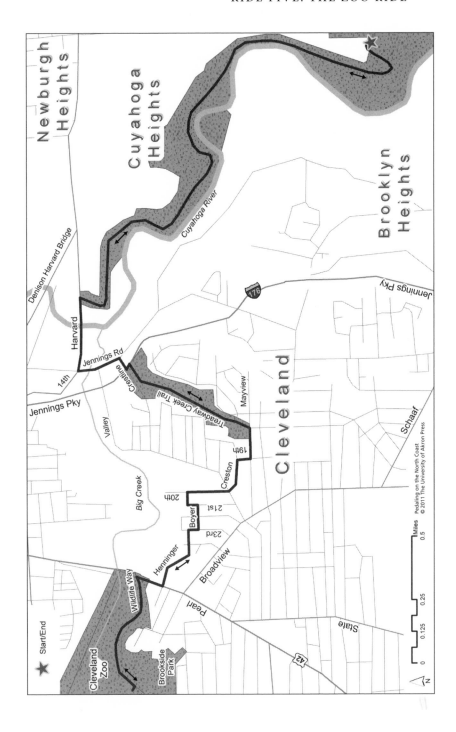

Ride 6

West Side Market

Route: Canal Visitor Center to West Side Market
Distance: 24 miles
Terrain: Mostly flat, with one hill outbound
Communities Visited: Independence, Valley View, Cuyahoga Heights, Cleveland
Starting/Ending Point: Canal Visitor Center, 7104 Canal Road, Independence, Ohio 44131
Points of Interest: Canal Visitor Center, Towpath Trail, Ohio & Erie Canal, historic Tremont neighborhood, Westside Market (Open Monday and Wednesday, 7 AM–4 PM; Friday–Saturday, 7 AM–6 PM)
How to Get There: Take I-77 to the Pleasant Valley exit (#153). Go east on Pleasant Valley and then north (left) on Brecksville Road/SR21. Turn east (right) Hillside Road. The Canal Visitor Center is on the right, just before Hillside Road ends at Canal Road.

Pedaling on the North Coast

T he West Side Market is a Cleveland landmark, and a visit there on a market day is a quintessential Cleveland experience. Housing over one hundred vendors representing a wide ethnic diversity, the market offers meats, seafood, vegetables, baked goods, dairy and cheese products, candy, nuts, and ready-to-eat foods in a multicultural environment. The markethouse, looking like a grand old train terminal, was actually built in 1912 to house the market, and it makes a great destination for this ride. On the way, you'll use part of the Towpath Trail, ride through historic Tremont, and have another unique Cleveland experience if you stop for lunch at Sokolowski's University Inn.

Murray, Tom, Scott, and I pick a Friday in April for this ride. This is a good day if you're planning on checking out the West Side Market, as it is open only on Mondays, Wednesdays, Fridays, and Saturdays. We meet at the Canal Visitor Center in Independence to start. As we unload our bikes, I see Murray has his Bruce Gordon BLT, Tom his Trek 830 Antelope, and Scott and I are on our Treks.

The Canal Visitor Center is located in Independence, in the Cuyahoga Valley National Park, at the intersection of Hillside Road and Canal Road. Independence is a residential and industrial suburb of Cleveland, incorporated as a village in 1914 and as city in 1960. Within ten square miles, Independence is both home to the largest open pit mine in Ohio and more than 1,300 acres in parkland. The mine is one of only a few in the country producing haydite, a low-unit-weight mineral used as an aggregate in lightweight structural concrete and other construction applications.

The displays in the visitor center illustrate the history of the canal: its construction, operation, decline, and ultimate restoration of the towpath as a recreational trail. We're familiar with the stories, although the displays are worth checking out if you are interested in learning more about the history of the towpath.

The Towpath Trail is on the west bank of the canal; we roll onto it and head north. The first couple of miles of the trail are paved with finely crushed limestone rather than asphalt, but that presents no problem for the bikes we are riding. Murray's, Tom's, and mine all have slightly wider tires than the average road bike, but even Scott's standard road tires, 700 x 25, roll easily enough on the dry limestone. Had we wanted to avoid the limestone surface, we could simply have crossed at the visitor center over to Canal Road, which parallels the towpath on the east side of the canal.

> **Changing Gears**
>
> Haydite, a lightweight aggregate used in structural concrete and masonry units, soil conditioners, landscaping mulch, and geotechnical fills, is not a naturally occurring material, but a manufactured product. After mining shale, it is "cooked" in a large, rotary kiln in the open-pit mine to convert it to haydite. Haydite has been used in many of Ohio's tall buildings, bridges, and sport arenas built within the last seventy years.

While in some other sections along the towpath the canal no longer exists, on this stretch, the channel looks much as it must have in the days when mule teams trudged on the trail, hauling packets and freight barges up and down the water route.

After a couple of miles of easy pedaling, we pass through a tunnel under Rockside Road, and we emerge to find some changes. First, the trail is blacktopped; those first two miles are the only unpaved miles on this route, and we will use them again on the return trip. Next, we are in another Cleveland suburb, Valley View, a residential and business community that was once part of Independence Township, but became its own village in 1919. Lastly, we have left the national park and are now in the Ohio & Erie Canal Reservation of the Cleveland Metroparks. The reservation is a narrow corridor of green space that follows a section of its namesake, making our journey through what is otherwise a commercial and industrial district a pleasure. At the south end of the reservation, where have entered, we can see company offices, restaurants, and other businesses to our left and right, but as we pedal northward, the corridor widens, so that the trees and foliage hide the surrounding urban landscape.

Just after we ride past the stanchions of the bridge carrying I-480 high above us, Murray's rear tire goes flat. He has an extra tube and an air pump for inflating it, so it's only a temporary inconvenience, but since Tom, Scott, and I seem compelled to offer Murray advice as he makes the repair, we prove the adage about the time required for a job increasing in direct correlation to the number of people supervising. But we finally get it done and start rolling again.

I rode this portion of the Towpath shortly after it opened, and there were two memorable interruptions where the trail crossed busy streets. They were inconvenient and jarring, as I had to stop, dismount, and wait for traffic lights to change. I am pleasantly surprised to find that now an attractive suspension bridge spans each of these intersections. The bridges were built expressly to convey the trail over the busy roads. Murray tells me that each one cost more than one million dollars. We pedal up and over them easily without stopping.

The trail passes under I-77, and at about that point, we enter Cuyahoga Heights, an industrial suburb of Cleveland, established as a village in 1918. On the trail, however, we view only continuing parkland. Nearing the north end of the reservation, we can see industrial sites beyond the trees, and though they are quiet now, their presence speaks of bygone days when steel-making and other heavy industry dominated the valley.

The Towpath Trail and the Metropark end at Harvard Avenue. There are plans to continue the trail to Lake Erie, but for now, we follow an alternative route. We turn left onto Harvard and cross the Cuyahoga River on a street-level bridge, entering Cleveland proper in the process. Then we turn right onto Jennings Road and follow it up a low rise. Ahead of us, we can see the lower edge of Steelyard Commons, a shopping center on the east side of Jennings Road, located on land formerly occupied by the No. 2 finishing mill of the LTV Corporation. The architecture of the center recalls the site's steelmaking heritage. The structure incorporates reclaimed steel framing and features salvaged artifacts of the halcyon days of big steel.

Before we reach the shopping center, however, Murray directs us to dismount, walk our bikes across a grass berm on our right, and enter a disused section of roadway where we remount. This short section leads us to a paved multi-use trail that runs behind Steelyard Commons, between the stores and an adjacent rail yard. A fence separates the trail from the rails and it's a smooth and pleasant path through an otherwise commercial and industrial area.

Once past the shopping center, the trail continues, passing by tunnel under Jennings Road and then under Quigley Road. Emerging on the north side of Quigley, the trail takes us up the hill to W. 14th Street, where it ends. We turn north on W. 14th and enter Tremont, a neighborhood of Cleveland's near west side. In the mid-nineteenth century, Tremont was known as Cleveland Heights and later, after the short-lived Cleveland University was started there, University Heights (both names were later taken by eastern suburbs). Even later, it became Lincoln Heights. With the construction of Tremont School in 1910, the neighborhood got its current name.

Rolling up W. 14th Street, we notice a sign as we cross Rowley Avenue. It points eastward and says "Christmas Story House." We can't see it from 14th, but we know the story. The structure is an ordinary house on W. 11th Street, around the corner from Rowley. It was the setting for the 1983 movie *A Christmas Story* (though supposedly set in Indiana). It's now open year-round for tours. A related museum sits across the street.

Continuing on W. 14th, we notice large churches on both sides of the street. In fact, Tremont is home to a large concentration of historic churches. Given the many nationalities repre-

---

Tremont

During the industrial boom, Tremont housed an eclectic mix of nationalities who worked in the mills. By 1994, according to one report, over thirty ethnic groups had lived or were then living in Tremont. But with the closing of mills and related industries in the 1980s, the district became rundown. Bridge closings and construction of I-71 and I-490 isolated the neighborhood. But Tremont's citizens fought back, organizing a development corporation to revitalize the area. Thus, by the 1990s, Tremont became known for its attractive park, good restaurants, coffee houses, rehabbed housing, and majestic churches. A growing artists' community helped to make Tremont a trendy place to live, and their presence explains the number of art galleries in the neighborhood.

sented over the years in the district, it's not surprising that while some of its houses of worship have spires, others have onion domes or round-capped towers.

We pass Lincoln Park on our right, a green rectangle that marks the heart of Tremont. Two blocks after that, we roll from W. 14th Street onto the entrance road to Abbey Avenue. We turn left on Abbey and cross a bridge over the low-ground banks of the Cuyahoga River, known as the "Flats." Once largely an industrial district, the Flats is now a mixed-use area, including industry, residences, and entertainment venues.

Soon thereafter, Abbey Road delivers us to an interchange with Lorain Avenue, across the street from the West Side Market. We cross Lorain at the light, chain our bikes to a fence next to the parking area, and head inside.

Crowded with shoppers, the market is a busy place. Having no way to transport foodstuffs back home, we don't shop for take-home items, but I feel duty bound to consume a cherry Danish and two chocolate-chip cannoli on the spot, and my comrades make similar sacrifices. And there is plenty to choose from: the counters are teeming with a wide variety of ethnic delicacies, baked goods, fresh meats, fish, and produce. While it isn't possible to identify the ethnicities represented in every booth, we spot separate vendors offering Hungarian, German, Czechoslovakian, Polish, Greek, Jewish, French, Italian, Irish, and Mexican foods. In addition, other booths categorize their wares more broadly, as Mediterranean, Middle Eastern, Hispanic, and so on. Walking the aisles, we notice items as varied as homemade pastas in numerous configurations and colors, Cajun crayfish raviolis, Hurka rice rings, crostatas, white chocolate raspberry mousse,

The West Side Markethouse

The market house was designed by architects Charles Hubbell and W. Dominick Benes, who also designed other famous buildings in Cleveland, including Shaker Heights High School, the Cleveland Museum of Art, the Mather Dance Center at Case Western Reserve University, and Wade Memorial Chapel in Cleveland's Lake View Cemetery.

Tremont's Historic W. 14th Street Churches

There are eight historic churches on W. 14th Street in Tremont. Here they are, from south to north:

- Zion United Church of Christ dates from 1867, when it was the German Evangelical Protestant Church. It moved to the present location in 1885, where the tall church is noted for its even taller steeple—175 feet. The church continued holding services exclusively in German until 1916, when one weekly English service was added. It later became part of the United Church of Christ through denominational merger.
- Pilgrim Congregational United Church of Christ. Though of the same denomination today as Zion UCC, Pilgrim, organized in 1859, came from Congregational Church roots. Its present building was opened in 1894, and features turrets and a 150-foot tower. Before 1894, the congregation worshiped in another edifice on W. 14th Street, the one now the home of St. Augustine Catholic Church.
- St. George Antiochian Orthodox Church was built in 1892 as the Lincoln Park Methodist Church. When the St. George congregation acquired the Romanesque structure, they added small onion domes to the base of the steeple to announce its "conversion" to Orthodoxy.
- El Calvario Pentecostal Church. This congregation makes its home in the former Emmanuel Evangelical United Brethren Church, which was built in 1908. That denomination had German roots. The current one has Hispanic ties.
- St. Augustine Roman Catholic Church occupies a red-brick Victorian building opened in 1870 as the home of the Pilgrim Congregational Church. The building was "re-baptized" Catholic after the Pilgrim congregation moved to its new quarters.
- Holy Ghost Byzantine Catholic Church, built in 1909, was a Cleveland landmark for one hundred years. The twin-domed structure was built by Ruthenian immigrants, eastern Slavic people from a region in the Carpathian Mountains. This church closed in 2009 because membership and funding were no longer sustaining. (The building actually fronts on Kenilworth Avenue, but is at the corner of Kenilworth and W. 14th Street.)
- St. Andrew Kim Korean Catholic Church. This tidy brick structure features a statue out front of the saint for which the church is currently named. The building was previously the home of Sacred Heart of Jesus Polish National Church.
- The Greek Orthodox Church of the Annunciation, built in 1913, was Cleveland's only Greek Orthodox Church until 1937. The brick edifice has twin towers with rounded caps.
- Other historic churches in Tremont, but not on W. 14th Street, include St. John Cantius Catholic Church, Sts. Peter and Paul Ukrainian Church, and St. Theodosius Russian Orthodox Cathedral.

roasted cauliflower, asparagus wrapped in speck, Cornish pasties, pistachio cheesecake, sheep cheese, sesame semolina bread, and bacon bark candy, just to name a few.

While savoring my second cannoli, I look up at the rounded arch ceiling, impressed by how artistic the concourse is compared to the utilitarian structures that house most modern stores. The market itself began in 1840 on its present location, but without benefit of a building, operating in the open. The markethouse, designed by the same architects who designed the Cleveland Museum of Art, opened in 1912 and includes a 137-foot clock tower that helps mark the edifice as a Cleveland landmark.

Having soaked up some of the marketplace ambiance, we retrieve our bikes and head back on Abbey Avenue. We will mostly retrace our route, but we make a small variation by turning left onto W. 13th Street and then onto University Road, where Sokolowski's University Inn, the lunch stop Tom had lobbied for, is located.

Once inside, I am surprised to find that the food is served cafeteria style, but it is definitely not "cafeteria food." The menu includes brats, sausages, kraut, potatoes, Salisbury steak, smoked kielbasa, pierogis, crab cakes, grilled sandwiches, hot vegetables, and much more. Tom orders a sausage and potato meal, Murray has a large salad with grilled chicken, Scott has brats and kraut, and I have a pastrami and cheese sandwich that is so filling that I almost wish I hadn't eaten the Danish and the cannoli. Almost. Murray calls Sokolowski's a Cleveland institution, and I can see—and taste—why.

Changing Gears

Sokolowski's University Inn
1201 University Road
(216) 771-9236
Sandwiches and entrees

Opened in 1923, the eatery is now run by the third generation of the Sokolowski family.

We exit the restaurant's parking lot at the rear, onto Abbey Avenue and then turn south on W. 14th Street. The return trip on the same route gives us an opportunity to get a second look at the interesting areas we covered on the way to the market.

Miles and Directions

Ride starts at Canal Visitor Center, 7104 Canal Road, Independence, Ohio 44131

0.0   Turn right out of Canal Visitor Center parking lot onto Hillside Road

0.1   Turn left onto Towpath Trail

2.0   Cross Old Rockside Road. Continue on Towpath Trail

7.9   Turn left onto West Harvard Avenue

8.2   Turn right onto Jennings Road

8.5   Cross Beltline Avenue. Immediately after Beltline, dismount and walk bike left, over curb and grass shoulder, to discontinued road. Proceed on discontinued road and enter multi-use trail. Stay on trail as it runs behind Steelyard Commons and then passes through two tunnels and climbs the hill beside Quigley Road

9.9   Turn right on W. 14th Street

11.0   Bear right to follow entrance road to Abbey Avenue

11.1   Turn left onto Abbey Avenue

11.7   Turn right onto Gehring Avenue and cross Lorain Avenue

11.8   Arrive at West Side Market

11.8   Backtrack across Lorain Avenue to Gehring Avenue

11.9   Turn left onto Abbey Avenue

12.4   Turn left onto W. 13th Street

12.5   Turn right onto University Road. Sokolowski's University Inn is on right

12.6   Exit Sokolowski's University Inn parking lot at rear, turning right onto Abbey Avenue

12.7   Turn left onto W. 14th Street entrance road. Then proceed straight onto W. 14th Street

13.9   Before W. 14th Street enters traffic circle, cross to sidewalk on left side of W. 14th Street. Follow sidewalk as it turns left and becomes multi-use trail. Stay on trail as it runs downhill beside Quigley Road, passes through two tunnels and continues behind Steelyard Commons

15.2   Trail ends at discontinued road. Proceed on discontinued road to end

15.3   At end of discontinued road, cross grass shoulder and turn left onto Jennings Road

15.6   Turn left onto West Harvard Avenue

15.9   Turn right into Towpath Trail parking lot and enter Towpath Trail

21.8   Cross Old Rockside Road

23.7   Turn right onto Hillside Road

23.8   Turn left into Canal Visitor Center parking lot

Ride 7
The Heights

Route: Beachwood to Cleveland Heights
Distance: 16 miles
Terrain: Mostly flat
Communities Visited: Beachwood, Shaker Heights, Cleveland Heights, University Heights, Pepper Pike
Starting/Ending Point: Mandel Jewish Community Center at 26001 S. Woodland Road Beachwood, OH 44122
Points of Interest: Maltz Museum of Jewish Heritage, historic mansions, Shaker Lakes, North and South Park Boulevards, Nature Center at Shaker Lakes, Ambler Heights Historic District, Alcazar Hotel, Coventry Village
How to Get There: Leave I-271 at exit 29. Turn west onto Chagrin Boulevard/US422. Turn right onto Richmond Road. Turn right onto South Woodland Road. The Mandel Center is just east of Richmond Road on the left side of South Woodland.

Although we've dubbed this ride The Heights, don't expect to do a lot of climbing. As bicycle routes go, this one is relatively flat. In general, "Heights" refers to the area east of Cleveland. Several communities sit on this plateau and take the moniker "Heights" from their location. The ride passes through three of these communities. The Heights has an average elevation of less than 1,000 feet, but you don't leave the plateau on this ride. At just over sixteen miles and with no significant climbing, this a great ride for average cyclists, though pros will enjoy it, too.

The Heights is a great homes tour; full of attractive, architecturally impressive residences, many built by wealthy owners in the late nineteenth and early twentieth centuries. University Heights actually bears the nickname "City of Beautiful Homes," but great homes, some even classifiable as "mansions," are strewn throughout this ride, along with more modest but equally pleasing neighborhoods.

The ride starts in Beachwood, at the Mandel Jewish Community Center on South Woodland Road, just east of the I-271 overpass.

Named for the beech trees that once covered a substantial part of the community, Beachwood reportedly got its current spelling because an early village clerk misspelled it on some official documents. Beachwood incorporated as a village in 1915, and attained city status in 1960.

It's a beautiful early spring day when Murray and I, along with Tom and Dave, saddle up in the parking lot of Mandel Center. We take a moment to look at Dave's steed. With its flat-crown fork, quill stem, cable-housing extending straight out of the brake levers, stem shifters, ten-speed gearing, and an orange paint job, we know immediately that we are looking at an old-timer, as bicycles go. It's a Fuji Special Tourer, which Dave tells us he's owned since it was new in 1975. He owns a couple of a newer bikes, but he's kept the old one primarily for riding bike trails paved only with crushed limestone, which tends to make bikes dirty quickly. Although we aren't cycling any trails on this ride, Dave is using the Fuji because, he sheepishly admits, he hasn't done the end-of-winter maintenance on the other ones yet. But the old bike is no problem. Properly cared for, bikes last for decades.

Murray is riding his Bruce Gordon BLT, a bicycle built for loaded touring (that is, the bicycle is loaded, not the rider!). Although his mount is overkill for this easy city ride, he likes its comfort and sturdy tires for bumping over city streets where maintenance is sometimes delayed. Tom is mounted on a Trek Antelope 830, an eighteen-speed mountain bike on which Tom has put road tires. I am riding my Specialized Sequoia.

We exit the parking lot and ride west on Woodland Road. As we cross Richmond Road, Tom points to the north and mentions that the Maltz Museum of Jewish Heritage is just up the street. The Maltz highlights the history and achievements of Cleveland's Jewish Community.

Although Woodland is a primary thoroughfare, the traffic on this two-lane street is moderate. We are able to pair up for conversation during the lulls between passing vehicles, and Murray and the guys act as informal tour guides.

By the time we cross Green Road, we have entered Shaker Heights. Each of the cities has its own history, but the residential areas appear so continuous that we have no sense of crossing boundaries as we roll from one community to another.

The homes along the first couple of miles of Woodland are modest and attractive. Once we cross Warrensville Road, however, mansions sit on both sides of the street. *The Ohio Guide*, published in 1940, described Shaker Heights as "a restricted community of expensive homes and estates, of landscaped lawns, lakes, and parks."

Someone once made the same point in shorthand, defacing a boundary sign to read "$haker Heights." More recently, however, the community has made concerted efforts toward integration, even setting up a loan fund for people buying homes.

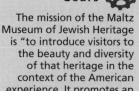

Changing Gears

The mission of the Maltz Museum of Jewish Heritage is "to introduce visitors to the beauty and diversity of that heritage in the context of the American experience. It promotes an understanding of Jewish history, religion and culture and builds bridges of appreciation, tolerance and understanding with those of other religions, races, cultures and ethnic backgrounds, serving as an educational resource for Northeast Ohio's Jewish and general communities."

Soon Murray directs us to turn right onto Eaton Road, which also boasts fine old residences. After a couple of blocks, we wheel across Shaker Boulevard and the adjacent tracks of the Rapid Transit line, reminding us that Shaker Heights developed as an inner-ring streetcar suburb of Cleveland.

A block farther, we turn left onto South Park Boulevard, a quiet street that borders the south edge of a significant stretch of forested parkland. Gorgeous homes sit across the street, facing the park. Continuing down the quiet drive, we approach a lake within the park. At the end, near an earthen dam, a roadside historic marker tells us about the "Shaker" part of the municipality's name. In 1822, a colony of the United Society of Believers, more commonly known as Shakers, established a community in the area. They dammed Doan Brook, creating two lakes, the one in front of us, called Horseshoe Lake (named for its shape), and another farther on called Lower Shaker Lake. The lakes harnessed waterpower to operate a woolen mill. The colony eventually faded and closed in 1889, in part due to the Shaker practice of celibacy. The land was sold and subsequently others developed Shaker Heights Village on the site, which was incorporated in 1912. It became a city in 1930. Today, about 70 percent of the com-

Horseshoe Lake

In 1822, Ralph Russell, a Connecticut pioneer who had settled in Warrensville Township ten years earlier, founded the North Union Shaker Community. The Shakers created Horseshoe Lake in 1852 when they built a dam across Doan Brook and harnessed its waterpower to operate a woolen mill near Lee Road and South Park Boulevard. The community disbanded in 1889; its 1,366 acres were eventually sold to a real estate syndicate from Buffalo, New York, the Shaker Heights Land Company. In 1896, this group deeded the Shaker Lakes Parklands to the City of Cleveland to preserve the green space in perpetuity. Ten years later, the Van Sweringen Company began to develop Shaker Heights Village as a Garden City suburb where William J. Van Aken served as mayor from 1915 until 1950. In the 1960s local residents successfully fought the proposed Clark Freeway, saving Horseshoe Lake and the Parklands from destruction.

From Ohio State Marker (Horseshoe Lake) located on South Park Boulevard in Shaker Heights, Ohio

munity is listed on the National Register of Historic Places as Shaker Village Historic District.

Murray grew up nearby, and while we are looking at the lake, he tells us that as a teenager, he and his friends came there to "watch submarine races." When he chuckles, we realize the expression is an old euphemism for parking after dark near the water with one's girlfriend.

We resume pedaling and soon pass the Nature Center at Shaker Lakes. It's an environmental education and preservation facility set up by local people in 1966 to keep the Shaker parklands from becoming the path of a freeway connecting Cleveland's East Side to downtown. Clearly, they succeeded, preserving the luscious green space through which we are wheeling. The center also maintains interpretive trails outside and nature displays inside.

A short distance farther on, South Park Boulevard merges with North Park Boulevard. We enter Cleveland Heights and cycle by more great homes. The parkland is now on our left, and we see Lower Shaker Lake through the trees.

The elevation of the plateau on which Cleveland Heights sits relative to Cleveland itself delayed settlement. The earliest settlers were farmers, followed by men who worked quarries on the plateau, but it wasn't until roads and later streetcar lines climbed the bluff that some of Cleveland's elite, wanting to escape the rapid expansion the big city, moved in and build large homes, especially in the western sections of the plateau-top. One of those elite, John D. Rockefeller, had large holdings throughout Cleveland Heights. As we can see from our bicycles, much of the fine architecture from those early days still stands.

Cleveland Heights officially became a hamlet in 1901, but two years later, after the state dropped that designation, it incorporated as a village. It became a city in 1921. Nineteen years after that, Cleveland Heights was as *The Ohio Guide* put it, "a city only in a political sense," and had become "a collection of neighborhoods on the highland… scattered over eight square miles [with] a half-dozen small business districts, all tending to reduce the large locality to a group of small ones." We visit three of these small business districts on this ride: Cedar-Fairmount, Coventry, and Cedar-Lee.

Presently, Murray shepherds us right onto Chestnut Hills Drive, which is one of the streets of a neighborhood officially designated Ambler Heights Historic District, but known to locals as Chestnut Hill. It was named for Dr. Nathan Hardy Ambler, a dentist who came to Cleveland in 1852, but the land wasn't acquired until several years after his death. Ambler's adopted son and nephew began the development. Ambler Heights contains only 73 acres, but no fewer than 112 buildings on them are designated "contributing properties" on the National Historic Register. Contributing properties are those that significantly add to the historical integrity or architectural qualities of a historic district. We quickly see that significance for ourselves as Murray steers us through a quick series of right and left turns weaving us up and down the streets of the neighborhood.

As we ride to the north end of Devonshire to rejoin Chestnut Hills Drive briefly, we approach a building that resembles a small castle. Tom tells us that this is Bicknell Mansion, built in the 1920s as the home of Cleveland businessman Warren G. Bicknell. Today, along with some newer adjacent structures, it comprises Judson Park, a continuing-care retirement facility. In its current life, Bicknell mansion houses seven apartments and its renovation earned an award from the Cleveland Restoration Society.

Completing our tour through Ambler Heights, we make a sharp right onto Cedar Road and enter one of those small business districts that characterize Cleveland Heights. This one is known locally as Cedar-Fairmount. Had we been ready to eat, there are options here, including a couple of coffee shops and Aladdin's Eatery, which features Lebanese-American cuisine, but we keep moving.

We wheel up Surrey and see on our right the five-story Alcazar Hotel, a Spanish/Moorish-style structure built in 1923 that quickly became a social-life hub. Entertainer Bob Hope, composer Cole Porter, and actor Johnny "Tarzan" Weissmuller all had residences in the Alcazar, which comes from an Arabic word meaning "home in a fortress." No longer a hotel, the Alcazar now operates as a senior residence, a bed and breakfast, and a corporate housing center. It's worth getting off your bike and going in to view the Alcazar's lobby.

Surrey Road takes us to Euclid Heights Boulevard, where we turn right. This pike has two lanes in each direction divided by a grassy, landscaped median. We ride single-file in the eastbound curb lane, heading toward Coventry Road.

Soon we come to the intersection with Coventry Road, and Murray directs us to pull our bikes to the curb. He, Tom and Dave are all familiar with the area, but Murray wants to tell me, as the newcomer, about the Coventry neighborhood, which contains another of the Cleveland Heights commercial districts. Pointing north up Coventry Road, Murray relates that the area, sometimes referred to as Cleveland's Greenwich Village, was the heart of the beat and alternative communities in the 1950s, '60s and '70s. Still a bustling district, Coventry Village offers an eclectic assortment of interesting stores and unique restaurants. Here, too, we could find lunch, whether we wanted Chinese, Japanese, Mongolian or Mexican food, or cuisine with American roots. Dave tells me that one of his all-time favorite eateries is on Coventry Road. It's called Tommy's, and in addition to a full standard menu, it offers vegan, vegetarian, macrobiotic, and gluten-free items. Tommy's launched as a soda fountain in 1972, and that year, *Rolling Stone* magazine named it the site of the "Best Milk shake East of the Mississippi." Those shakes are still available at Tommy's, Dave says.

But for our lunch today, Murray has somewhere else in mind, so we don't take the side trip down Coventry Road. (If you do, we suggest you dismount and walk your bike on the sidewalk. It's a good idea to avoid riding on sidewalks unless absolutely necessary; local police are known to ticket for riding on the sidewalk.)

Instead, we cross Coventry Road as pedestrians and head into the green space on the opposite corner that is Coventry Peace Park. We walk under the gateway arch designed out of industrial piping, climb back on our steeds and roll the short distance to the end of the walkway and onto Washington Boulevard. This is a quiet neighborhood street with a grassy median. We follow Washington to Cottage Grove Avenue, stay on it across Cedar Road and then turn left onto Meadowbrook Boulevard. This leads us to Lee Road and lunch, in yet another small business district, called Cedar-Lee, which is famous for its theatre of the same name. The Cedar Lee Theatre is a Cleveland Heights landmark, a popular place to see independent and foreign films as well as some Hollywood flicks in a traditional theatre environment. From the intersection of Meadowbrook and Lee, the theatre is a block north.

We, however, are looking to eat, not to catch a movie, so we look south to see the Stone Oven Bakery and Café a half block down on the opposite side of the street. Following Murray, we proceed across Lee and turn right into the parking lot behind the block of shops. At the rear entrance to the Stone Oven, we find a good place to park our bikes.

The Stone Oven, Murray tells us, is one of the top three bakeries in Northeast Ohio, but inside, the gourmet sandwiches, salads and soups, along with a wide assortment of European-style pastries and cookies, speak for themselves. Murray goes for chicken-salad on pita bread; Dave for an eggplant, zucchini and red pepper sandwich with a side of couscous; and Tom for black-bean soup. I select a slice of a vegetable pizza with tabouli on the side. I've never had tabouli before and find that it tastes as good as it looks. When I inquire, I learn it's a traditional Lebanese dish, a mix of bulgur, chopped vegetables, and spices. The wide selection of food in the Coventry and Cedar-Lee area makes it easy to discover new dishes every time you ride this route.

Changing Gears

Stone Oven
2267 Lee Road
(216) 932-3003

We share a table by the front window, and Dave tells me to notice the parking meters outside. Colorful twine, crocheted into patterns, encircles the post of each one, bringing an arty flair to the street. After lunch, I see that the posts out back are similarly adorned.

While we are eating, a woman—younger than any of us—approaches our table and cheerfully greets Murray, and the two engage in a moment of friendly conversation. After she moves on to the food line, Tom, with sly smile, says, "It rare to ride with Murray and *not* have a woman accost him somewhere along the way." We enjoy the comment at Murray's expense, but in fact, Murray does seem to have friends all over Greater Cleveland.

As we finish up, Murray gets in the deli line again to buy a peanut-butter cookie. He later tells me that he and his late wife had a rating system for such treats, a scale of 1 to 5, with 5 being the best. This cookie, Murray says, is at least a 4.

Stomachs full, we head south briefly on Lee Road and then follow a series of streets through a blue-collar neighborhood and enter University Heights. This community was part of Warrensville Township until 1908, when it incorporated as a village named Idlewood. The villagers adopted the present name in 1925 when John Carroll University moved in. The school, in turn, attracted more residents, and by 1940, University Heights became a city.

Our ride passes within a few blocks of the college, but we are not near enough to see the campus.

Eventually our route takes us south across Fairmount Boulevard to Shelburne Road where we resume our eastward tack. Shelburne parallels Fairmount and is a low-traffic residential street. The Shelburne neighborhood looks prosperous and the houses are attractive, but of more recent vintage than the old mansions.

After a few blocks, we cross back into Beachwood. Where Shelburne ends, we bear left onto Laureldale Road, which quickly brings us to Fairmount Boulevard, on which we continue east. There's a bit more traffic on Fairmount, but not so much as to make cycling unreasonable. We stay on Fairmount across Richmond Road and shortly thereafter cross over I-271, which marks our entry into Pepper Pike, which became a village in 1924. The origin of the name is uncertain, but one version has it that it came from a family named Pepper who lived beside the area's primary thoroughfare, a turnpike. It became a city in 1970. On this ride, we traverse only the western edge of the community.

The intersection beyond the I-271 overpass is Brainard Road. We follow that south to a traffic circle, which we enter, flowing with the minimal traffic around the right-hand side. Murray has previously alerted us to watch for a sidewalk turnoff on the south end of the circle. We turn right onto it, which takes us onto a short driveway that leads us onto Old Brainard Road.

As we pedal along, Dave mentions that he's been working with a group that helps reintegrate former prisoners into society and he's been thinking about seeing if one of those individuals would like to have his Fuji. (Indeed, the next time Dave joins Murray, Tom and I for a ride, he's on a different set of wheels. A former inmate is using "old orange" for his transportation needs.)

Soon we come to South Woodland Road. We turn right and pass under I-271. A few strokes of our pedals beyond that bring us full circle, back to the Mandel Center, completing our pleasurable tour.

Miles and Directions

The ride starts at the Mandel Jewish Community Center at 26001 S. Woodland Road, Beachwood, Ohio. The Center is just east of Richmond Road on the north side of S. Woodland.

0.0	Exit Mandel Jewish Community Center parking area, turning right onto S. Woodland Road
0.4	Cross Richmond Road
1.2	Cross Green Road
2.2	Cross Warrensville Road
2.9	Turn right onto Eaton Road
3.2	Cross Shaker Boulevard
3.3	Turn left onto South Park Boulevard
3.9	Horseshoe Lake marker, on right
4.3	Bear right at intersection, staying on South Park Boulevard
4.6	Nature Center at Shaker Lakes on left
4.8	Cross Woodland Road as South Park merges with North Park Boulevard. Continue on N. Park Boulevard
6.5	Turn right onto Chestnut Hills Drive (enter Ambler Heights Historic District)
6.6	Turn right onto Denton Drive
6.7	Turn left onto Devonshire Drive
6.8	Turn right onto Chestnut Hills Drive
6.9	Turn right onto Elandon Drive
7.0	Turn left onto Denton Drive
7.1	Turn left onto Harcourt Drive
7.5	Turn a sharp right onto Cedar Road
7.7	Turn left onto Surrey Road. CAUTION: Heavy traffic area. We suggest you dismount and cross Cedar Road at the traffic light at Grandview Avenue, and walk to Surrey
7.9	Turn right onto Euclid Heights Boulevard
8.7	Cross Coventry Road to the corner park with the arch. (Coventry Area, which includes restaurants and shops, is to the left, on Coventry Road). Pass under the arch and follow path onto Washington Boulevard
9.3	Turn right onto Cottage Grove Avenue

9.4   Cross Cedar Road

9.5   Turn left onto Meadowbrook Boulevard

9.8   Turn right onto Lee Road (The Stone Oven Bakery and Café is a half block south on Lee Road, on the left. For bicycle parking, we suggest continue across Lee Road on Meadowbrook and turn right behind the shops to the rear entrance of The Stone Oven)

9.8   Continue south on Lee Road

10.1   Turn left on East Scarborough Road

10.5   Jog right onto Taylor Road then left onto the continuation of East Scarborough

10.9   Turn right onto Canterbury Road

11.1   Turn left onto Bradford Road

11.2   Turn right onto Eaton Road

11.5   Cross Fairmount Boulevard

11.6   Turn left onto Shelburne Road

12.2   Cross Warrensville Road

13.1   Cross Green Road

13.6   Bear left onto Laureldale Road

13.7   Turn right onto Fairmount Boulevard

14.2   Cross Richmond Road

14.8   Cross over I-271

15.0   Turn right onto Brainard Road

15.4   Enter traffic circle, following it around the left side

15.6   On south side of circle, turn right onto path to Old Brainard Road

15.7   Head south on Old Brainard Road

15.9   Turn right onto South Woodland Road

16.3   Turn right into Mandel Jewish Community Center parking area

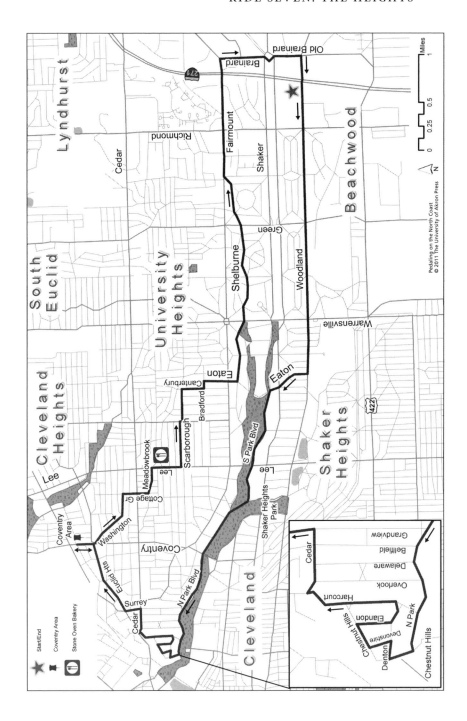

Pedaling on the North Coast
© 2011 The University of Akron Press

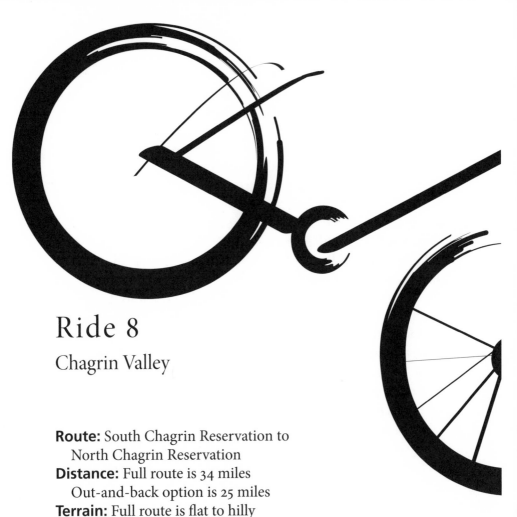

Ride 8

Chagrin Valley

Route: South Chagrin Reservation to
 North Chagrin Reservation
Distance: Full route is 34 miles
 Out-and-back option is 25 miles
Terrain: Full route is flat to hilly
 Out-and-back option is flat to rolling
Communities Visited: Moreland Hills, Hunting Valley,
 Gates Mills, Mayfield Heights, Pepper Pike
Starting/Ending Point: Parking lot in South Chagrin
 Reservation near intersection of Chagrin River Road and
 Sulphur Springs Drive (just south of Miles Road)
Points of Interest: Chagrin Falls, Chagrin River, polo field,
 Hunting Valley, Gates Mills, Squire's Castle
How to Get There: From I-480 east, take the Miles Road
 exit toward North Randall/Bedford Heights. Turn slight
 right onto Miles Road. Follow it to Chagrin River Road.
 Turn left onto Chagrin River Road, proceed to parking
 area.

Pedaling on the North Coast

This ride travels on the easternmost continuous road in Cuyahoga County. Named for the watercourse with which it shares a scenic valley, Chagrin River Road winds from South Chagrin Reservation through picturesque horse country to North Chagrin Reservation, where it crosses into Lake County and leads to Squire's Castle, the ruins of a rich man's retreat. Outbound, the route passes through rural areas of Moreland Hills, Hunting Valley, Gates Mills and Willoughby Hills. The return path enters the quaint village area of Gates Mills and then climbs out of the valley to pass through suburban areas of Mayfield Heights and Pepper Pike before plunging back down to the valley floor.

Those who prefer a shorter ride and one without the two climbs on the full route can still enjoy the primary feature of this journey—the Chagrin Valley. Just stay on Chagrin River Road from the start point to Squire's Castle and then return by the same route. (The ride narrated here is the full-route, but it also covers all of the ground you'll pedal if you use the shorter out-and-back option.)

This is a good ride for a picnic lunch, as food options are limited. There are no places to purchase snacks on the route itself, so make sure to bring some along. Gates Mills features a highly regarded restaurant called Sara's Place, which would welcome you even in bicycle garb, but it's more of a fine-dining experience than you may want while on a bike outing. But the Squire's Castle picnic area at the turnaround point is a great spot to stop for a pleasant lunch in the park. Alternatively, there are several restaurant choices in the village of Chagrin Falls, less than two miles from the start/end point of the ride.

Murray, Tom, Wayne and I pedal the Chagrin Valley ride on a chilly but pleasant spring day. Although we've mentioned Wayne on a previous ride, this ride is the first one Wayne rode with us. While he is my frequent riding companion, neither

Changing Gears

Dining in Chagrin Falls:

Fresh Start Diner
16 North Main Street
(440) 893-9599
Sandwiches, wraps, and salads; breakfast available all day

Yours Truly Restaurant
30 North Main Street
(440) 247-3232
Sandwiches, salads, omelets, entrees

Joey's Restaurant
44 North Main Street
(440) 247-6085
Italian food

Murray nor Tom has met him before today. Wayne is seventy-six, but rides like someone much younger, and his bicycle gives him an added advantage. It's a Trek Pilot 5.0, with a carbon-fiber frame. That means it's lighter than any of ours, and is therefore less weight for him to push along. Murray is riding his Bruce Gordon touring bike and Tom is today mounted on his Surly CrossCheck, an all-purpose bike that's often sold for commuting and light touring. My Specialized Sequoia is the nearest match to Wayne's Trek. It has a carbon-fiber fork and rear stays but the main triangle of the frame is aluminum, which isn't quite as light. Once we are on the road, however, it's not about what bikes we're riding; it's about the joy of pedaling a great route with good friends.

After leaving our vehicles in a parking area just south of Miles Road in South Chagrin Reservation, we cross Miles and roll onto Chagrin River Road, heading north. Murray tells us to ride single file, stating that local laws require it and the police enforce it. We soon see a sign that states the single file rule as well, and I can see why it's a good idea; though the traffic is not heavy, the road is narrow and without paved shoulders.

Almost right away, a roadside sign tells us we are in Moreland Hills and that it was the birthplace of James Garfield, the twentieth president of the United States. Though we won't see

President James A. Garfield

James A. Garfield, twentieth president of the United States, was born in 1831 in Orange Township (which became Moreland Hills, Ohio, in 1929). Though his father died when he was two, his family remained on the farm, where Garfield helped as he grew older. He remained there through his young working years as a canal boat driver and while he attended Geauga Seminary and Hiram Eclectic Institute (which later became Hiram College). He left the area to attend Williams College in Massachusetts, from which he graduated in 1856, but returned to Ohio to teach the classics at his Hiram alma mater. Within a year, he became president of the school, and in 1859, was elected to the Ohio Senate. He served in the Union army during the Civil War, rising to the rank of major general, and was then elected to Congress, where he remained until elected president in 1880. He took office in 1881, but served only two hundred days as president before being assassinated by an unsuccessful federal office seeker.

it on this route, the log cabin in which Garfield was born still stands, a couple of miles west of where we are, over on SR91, near the Moreland Hills government offices.

We soon come to a polo field that is part of the South Chagrin Reservation. There's no activity on the grounds at this moment, but looking at it, I realize that I've never seen a polo field before, except on TV or in the movies. It seems to fit right in here, however, because although we are in a rural suburb—only 3200 residents in the eight square miles of Moreland Hills—it is not devoted to farming. Rather it features fields and forests, complete with bridle paths. And several of the homesteads we pass have stables and the wood fences typical of horse paddocks.

Continuing, we cross SR87 and exit South Chagrin Reservation. We pedal into Hunting Valley, another village of eight square miles, but this one has only 750 residents, living in attractive country estates and pastoral splendor. The website for the village, incorporated in 1924, indicates that its "hiking trails, polo fields and bridle paths... [suggest] life in a more peaceful and unspoiled past."

Crossing Cedar Road, we enter Gates Mills, formed in 1826. A continuation of the pastoral scene, this community of just under nine square miles has 2,500 residents. Since we began this ride, the Chagrin River has been on our right, east of the road, though seldom visible from the pavement. As we come near the village center of Gates Mills, however, we see the river, and then cross a bridge where the river shifts to the left side of the road. The village center is on both sides of the river, and we are quickly through it. As we continue northward, we pass several older but well-kept homes. We soon enter North Chagrin Reservation and shortly thereafter, cross another bridge as the river moves back to the east side of the road; it will stay on that side for the remainder of our outbound ride. According to one story, the Chagrin River was named by Moses Cleaveland, the founder of Cleveland, to express embarrassment after he and his surveyors followed it for several miles before realizing that it was not the Cuyahoga River.

Immediately after the bridge, Wilson Mills Road intersects with Chagrin River Road from the left. We turn onto it and almost right away, turn right into a Metropark trailhead. Here, after wheeling through the parking lot, we roll onto a black-topped multi-purpose trail that soon has us climbing through a scenic gorge. To this point, we have all been riding at about the same pace, but the steep hill soon sorts us out. Every cyclist has his or her own preferred climbing mode. Some like to gear down and ascend slowly but steadily upward. Some would rather stay in higher gears and stand up on the pedals. Some choose mid-range gears but crank harder from a seated position. Others use some combination of these methods, especially on longer hills. In most cases, it's understood without saying that everyone should get up the hill using the technique that they are most comfortable with.

In the case of us four, Wayne climbs seemingly without breaking a sweat. Tom is not far behind him. I'm a little further back and Murray, climbing steadily, brings up the rear. When Murray catches up to me, he speaks admiringly of Wayne's uphill prowess, and tells me, with a twinkle in his eye, that Wayne is his "new hero."

At the top of the bike path, we turn right onto an unsigned park road, which takes us through more forest and eventually by some picnic areas with pavilions. Coming to a junction, we turn right onto Ox Lane. It's flat at first, but soon has us rolling downhill to an intersection where we make a sharp left, continuing on Ox Lane. Spinning a little further, we come Chagrin River Road again, but north of where we left it. We turn left, and after a few moments, cross into Lake County. We are still in the North Chagrin Reservation, but the community around it is Willoughby Hills (a village in 1954 and a city in 1970).

About a mile further on, we come to the Squire's Castle picnic area on the left. The building for which the site is named, though set well back from the road, is clearly visible and does, in fact, look like a castle. But it wasn't intended to be. Rather, in the 1890s, Feargus B. Squire, a Standard Oil magnate, built the stone structure with a three-story tower and an even taller turret as the gatekeeper's house for his planned country estate. As things worked out, Squire never built the estate, but he used the gatehouse for a weekend retreat from time to time. It's now owned by the Metroparks.

Leaving the bikes near the path that leads to the castle, we walk to it and go inside. The doors and windows are gone and the building is a shell with the roof and upper flooring missing from the tower section. But the walls, floors and remaining roofs are solid and the structure is open to the public. Roaming inside and reading the informative plaques about the building and Squire himself gives us a feel of what the home once was.

I see that it is also a place where children can let their imaginations have free rein, as a few are apparently doing during our visit, judging from the excited way they point at the turret and chatter at their parents.

After enjoying some snacks from our bike bags, we remount and head south, taking Chagrin River Road back into Cuyahoga County and continuing as far as the center of Gates Mills. Just before the highway bridge, we cross the river on a footbridge that takes us into the west bank part of the village center. At the end of the bridge, we are facing the Chagrin Valley Hunt Club. Our path through this charming hamlet takes us behind the club were we see several horses and riders going through their paces in a fenced enclosure.

As we head away from the village center on Epping Road, every house we see (with the exception of one made of stone) is painted a gleaming white. Though each house is unique, the uniformity of color makes us wonder if there is a zoning rule about it. We come to the junction with Berkshire Road, turn right and climb for eight-tenths of mile. After it levels out, we continue on Berkshire to where it ends at Old Mill Road. There, we turn left and almost immediately, swing left again and onto Gates Mills Boulevard.

This thoroughfare is a four-lane drive with the opposing lanes of traffic divided by a landscaped median strip, though at first this strip is so wide and wooded that we can't see the lanes for the opposing traffic. The road passes through a suburban residential area and is not heavily traveled. We pedal in the right-hand lane, and what vehicles there are obligingly pass on our left without crowding us.

We stay on this boulevard for just over four miles, running southwest. Three times, we find it interrupted by traffic circles where other roads cross. At the first, we pass into Mayfield Heights, but are only in it momentarily as we roll diagonally through a suburban slice of the community.

By the second circle, we are well into Pepper Pike. Though an affluent suburb today, it was still rural at the end of the nineteenth century. But in 1897, the Chagrin Falls-Cleveland interurban railway was built through the township, which made the area accessible to downtown Cleveland, and spurred development. Subsequent road building, especially including nearby I-271, boosted growth.

The third of the traffic roundabouts is Shaker Circle, where we travel more than three-fourths of the way around it to turn east on Shaker Boulevard, right in front of the Pepper Pike city building. Shaker Boulevard, lined with still more tasteful homes, ends with swift down slope, delivering us once more to Chagrin River Road. From there, we retrace our outbound path.

Feargus Squire

Feargus B. Squire, who built Squire's Castle in the 1890s, was a vice president at Standard Oil Company. He'd come to the United States in 1860 from Exeter, England, at age ten. Starting as an office boy for an oil company, he joined Standard Oil of Ohio in 1885, as co-manager with Frank Rockefeller, John D. Rockefeller's brother, and eventually rose to vice president. One of his major achievements at Standard Oil was developing the first tank wagon for oil shipment.

In 1890, Squire bought 525 acres in what is now North Chagrin Reservation, intending to build a large estate home. The building now known as Squire's Castle was designed to be the gatekeeper's lodge for the estate, but Squire's plans changed, and the estate was never built. He instead used the gatehouse for a weekend and summer retreat.

Squire retired from Standard Oil in 1909. In 1922, he sold the property that included the castle, and the Metroparks system acquired it in 1925. Squire died in 1932.

As we approach the crossing with SR87, Wayne is in the lead, and I am several yards behind him. As he passes under the traffic signal, it changes to yellow, so I stop. Wayne is soon out of sight. Presently, Tom and Murray arrive, and Murray asks me, "Where's Lance?" He knows a gifted rider when he sees one.

The light changes and we three proceed and soon see "Lance," who has dawdled to let us catch up. We continue in companionable silence, enjoying the forested surroundings of the final miles of this great ride.

Miles and Directions
Full Route

0.0	From parking lot, cross Sulphur Springs Drive
0.1	Cross Miles Road and head north on Chagrin River Road (only single-file riding permitted on Chagrin River Road)
1.5	Cross Chagrin Boulevard
2.8	Cross S. Woodland Road
3.9	Cross Shaker Boulevard
5.1	Cross Fairmount Boulevard
5.9	Cross Cedar Road
7.4	Turn right with Chagrin River Road (just beyond Gates Mills Historical Society) and cross bridge. Then turn left to stay on Chagrin River Road, which is also SR174
8.4	Cross Mayfield Road
9.9	Turn left on Wilson Mills Road
10.0	Turn right onto Metro Parks Drive and enter paved trail
10.7	Turn right onto unsigned Metroparks road
11.8	Turn right onto Ox Lane
12.6	Turn hairpin left to stay on Ox Lane
13.0	Turn left onto Chagrin River Road
13.9	Turn left into Squire's Castle Picnic and proceed to end of parking lot, toward castle
14.1	Walkway to Squire's Castle
14.1	Return through parking lot to picnic area entrance
14.3	Turn right onto Chagrin River Road
16.7	Cross Wilson Mills Road
18.2	Cross Mayfield Road
19.0	Turn right onto footbridge in Gates Mills (just after Sara's Place restaurant on left and just before Mayer Insurance office on right)
19.1	Turn right onto Old Mill Road
19.15	Turn left onto Epping Road
20.0	Turn right onto Berkshire Road
21.3	Turn left onto Old Mill Road

21.4 Turn left onto Gates Mills Boulevard.
CAUTION: The NE bound lane is right next to Berkshire Road across a grassy strip. You want the SW bound lane, which you enter from Old Mill Road

22.5 Travel right half way around SOM Center Circle and continue on Gates Mills Boulevard

23.3 Cross Cedar Road

24.2 Travel right half way around Fairmount Circle and continue on Gates Mills Boulevard

26.6 Travel right around Shaker Circle. At bottom of circle, turn left onto Shaker Boulevard, East

26.9 Turn right out of circle onto Shaker Boulevard, East

29.9 Turn right onto Chagrin River Road

30.9 Cross Woodland Road

32.3 Cross Chagrin Road

33.7 Cross Miles Road and enter parking area

33.8 Cross Sulphur Springs Drive

To visit Village of Chagrin Falls

0.0 Leave parking area, turning right onto Miles Road

1.3 Turn left onto Solon Road

1.4 Turn right onto Maple Street

1.6 Turn left onto Franklin Street

1.7 Turn right onto Washington Street and then left onto Main Street (food at Main Street Diner, Yours Truly, Joey's, Einstein Bagels, Falls Ice Cream and Candy Shop)

Out-and-Back Route

0.0 From parking lot, cross Sulphur Springs Drive

0.1 Cross Miles Road and head north on Chagrin River Road (only single-file riding permitted on Chagrin River Road)

1.5 Cross Chagrin Boulevard

2.8 Cross S. Woodland Road

3.9 Cross Shaker Boulevard

5.1 Cross Fairmount Boulevard

5.9 Cross Cedar Road

7.4   Turn right with Chagrin River Road (just beyond Gates Mills Historical Society) and cross bridge. Then turn left to stay on Chagrin River Road, which is also SR174

8.4   Cross Mayfield Road

9.9   Turn left on Wilson Mills Road

12.3   Turn left into Squire's Castle Picnic and proceed to end of parking lot, toward castle

12.5   Walkway to Squire's Castle
After visiting Squire's Castle, return via same route to start point

24.9   Cross Miles Road and enter parking area

25.0   Cross Sulphur Springs Drive

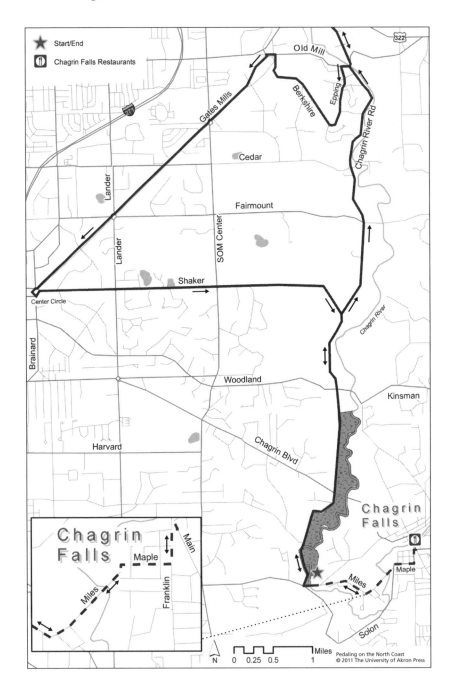

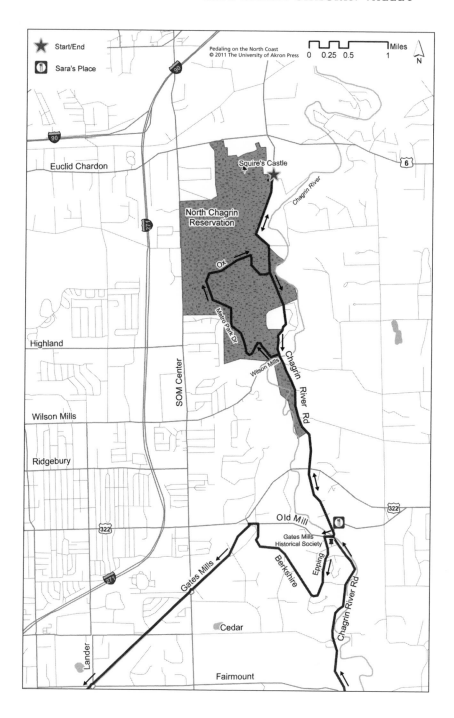

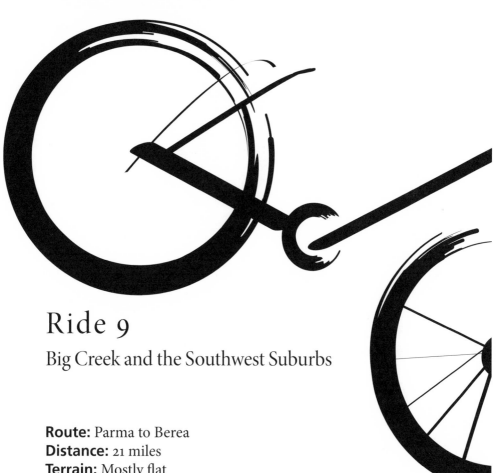

Ride 9
Big Creek and the Southwest Suburbs

Route: Parma to Berea
Distance: 21 miles
Terrain: Mostly flat
Communities Visited: Parma, Parma Heights, Middleburg
  Heights, Strongsville, Berea
Starting/Ending Point: Lower Fern Hill Picnic Area on Big
  Creek Parkway, just south of Brookpark Road
Points of Interest: Big Creek Reservation, Mill Stream Run
  Reservation, Whitney Road covered bridge, Berea square,
  Victorian homes on S. Rocky River Drive
How to Get There: Take I-480 to Tiedeman Road. Go south
  on Tiedeman to Brookpark Road. Turn left on Brookpark
  then right on Big Creek Parkway, then right into Lower
  Fern Hill Picnic Area.

If you're looking for a friendly ride that's interesting but not too demanding, this is it. It's mostly flat and the largest part of it can be ridden on a paved multi-purpose trail through wooded parkland. Even where there is no trail, the roads are lightly traveled, and those who want to move faster can pedal the whole route on road.

The route is a combination of a loop and an out-and-back route. On the map, its profile is a constellation—a "little dipper" with a somewhat mangled cup. Most of the miles are in Big Creek Reservation, which is part of the Cleveland Metroparks system, but it also wanders through two different sections of Mill Stream Run Reservation, and five of Cleveland's southwest suburbs. The feel of the trip is more park than city, however.

On a hot morning in July, Murray, Tom, Dave, Wayne and I gather at Lower Fern Hill Picnic Area at the north of Big Creek Parkway. We are all riding road bikes but they are different models and vintages, from Murray's Bianchi to Tom's Surly. Our eclectic mix reminds us that, no matter what bikes we use, we are here to cycle with friends and explore Greater Cleveland together.

Although an excellent paved, multi-purpose trail parallels the parkway and a good bit of the rest of the ride, we have opted to pedal on the roadways. This is not due to any shortcoming of the trail, but because the road presents fewer reasons to slow down. The trail is shared with pedestrians, dog-walkers, and even skaters, and we're leaving the trail to them. We exit the picnic area at its east end, turning south on the parkway. (If you do decide to use the trail, head for the west end of the picnic area, where you'll cross a small footbridge and join the trail).

One of the first things I notice is that although Big Creek is a Reservation of the Metroparks system, it doesn't contain as much parkland as some of the other parks. Much of Big Creek is a green corridor but this parkway also serves as a residential street. Some sections have houses on one side of the road and parkland on the other. Big Creek is a long, skinny park and in some sections it's little wider than the road itself. Nonetheless, it still has that "park feel" and it really shines when it spreads out a bit.

While still at the north end of the reservation, we are within the city of Parma, Cleveland's largest suburb by population—over 85,000 at the 2000 census. Several of the suburb cities in this part of Cuyahoga County experienced a population boom after World War II, gradually transforming the area from rural to suburban, and Parma is no exception. The community was formed from a township of the same name, reportedly borrowing the name from Parma, New York. In turn, the New York Parmaites likely took the name from the Italian community of that name during the early nineteenth century. Ohio's Parma incorporated as a village in 1924, a city in 1931, and had its biggest growth in the post-WW II era.

Another difference between Big Creek Parkway and other roads in the Metroparks is that it has more grade-level cross streets. But the minor ones have little traffic and the major ones have traffic lights, so they are all easy to get across.

As we traverse the first of those major streets, Snow Road, we move from Parma into Parma Heights, a community that broke from Parma Township in 1912. It became a city in 1959.

When we cross W. 130th Street, we enter Middleburg Heights, which was once the onion capital of the nation. The township incorporated as village in the 1920s and became the City of Middleburg Heights in 1961.

We cruise under a bridge for the I-71 interstate highway and pass a large cemetery on our right. It, plus a library and an ele-

Middleburg Heights

When the first European settlers arrived in the area that would become Middleburg Heights, they found it contained a large swamp, which they named Podunk. They soon realized that its black muck would be good for growing vegetables if they could lower the water level. Around 1843, they used hand shovels to widen an existing stream and increase the drainage from the swamp, exposing acres of black earth on which they planted produce, especially onions. Sometime thereafter, Middleburg Township earned the reputation as the onion capital of the nation.

Following World War II, as population grew in the whole area, the demand for housing in Middleburg Heights eventually overtook the farms. The last farm ceased operations ten years later.

mentary school, are the only non-residential properties I have noticed along the parkway.

We next cross Fowles Road and see a large tract of land on the west side of the road. Some of this is covered by Lake Isaac, which along with the nearby Beyer Pond, form the heart of Lake Isaac Waterfowl Sanctuary. A paved trail extends about three miles from Lake Isaac to a trailhead on Eastland Road near Lake Abram. Lake Isaac and Lake Abram are the two largest remaining glacial pothole wetlands in Cuyahoga County.

A short distance south of Lake Isaac, we pass Main Street, and roll into Strongsville, still within the park. John S. Strong, a New Englander who arrived in the area in 1816, is the source of the community's name. It became a village in 1927 and a city in 1960.

We soon roll downhill into the Rocky River valley, crossing by a bridge over the Ohio Turnpike and streaming past woodlands on the way. Big Creek Parkway ends at Valley Parkway within Mill Stream Run Reservation. We turn right onto Valley Parkway, pass almost immediately under a bridge carrying the turnpike, and then turn left onto Whitney Road and cross the Rocky River on a covered bridge. At some other times of year, the river runs strong and churns, but now, in the middle of a dry summer, it's a quiet stream.

Changing Gears

The Ohio Turnpike played an important role in the development of Strongsville. In 1955, When that highway opened in the area, developers purchased a lot of the land, ending most of the farming. In the 1960s, I-71 came through the community as well, meaning that Strongsville was now at the crossing of two major highways, one running east-west and one running north-south. Seeing opportunity, the city launched an aggressive and successful program to bring more industries within its borders.

A short distance further, we follow Whitney as it makes a left-hand turn, becoming Eastland Road in the process, and we pass under the turnpike once more. We turn right onto Fair Road, leave the park and enter a residential area. Eventually, we make a couple more right turns and cross the turnpike a fourth time, now above it on the Sprague Road bridge. Because of the bridges and underpasses, however, we've have little sense of being near a busy superslab.

Once over the highway, we turn left off Sprague, and enter a residential part of Berea. From around 1840 and continuing for about one hundred years, Berea thrived by cutting building blocks and grindstones from the banks of the Rocky River, which explains its name. The excavating days are over, but they've left an imprint on the name of two roads on this ride: North Quarry Lane and South Quarry Lane.

Changing Gears

Café Ah-Roma
38 West Bridge Street
(440) 260-0286
Coffee, sandwiches

A few more turns through neighborhood streets brings us back into Mill Stream Run Reservation via South Quarry Lane, where we spin northward on Valley Parkway to the junction with North Quarry Lane. We follow this up a short, easy hill out of the valley to a shopping area of Berea. There, Murray directs us to the Café Ah-Roma, which features a selection of coffee drinks as well as sandwiches on homemade breads and vegetarian and vegan items.

We are not yet ready for lunch, but we head inside for drinks and snacks, most of us opting for coffee and bagels. As much as we enjoy riding, sitting down with fellow cyclists for good conversation over coffee is just as fun. We are all "of an age"—Dave, Tom and I are in our mid-60s; Murray and Wayne are in their 70s. But we are all active cyclists, and we all log plenty of miles annually, which keeps us feeling young. As we eat our blueberry bagels and sip our French Roast, we compare notes on how we each tally our annual bicycle mileage. At 7,500 miles, Wayne had the most last year. He tells us that while visiting the doctor's office recently for a routine matter, a the new nurse took his pulse and then called in another nurse to see if she was mistaken; she'd clocked Wayne's resting heart rate at only 40. We weren't surprised, however, for we'd had similar experiences. The frequent and vigorous exercise on our bikes has made our hearts more efficient, resulting in a slower pulse.

That cycling keeps us young came up in another way in a previous conversation I'd had with Murray. He is a widower, and he told me that he had signed onto Match.com, a dating website. But he said, "I don't think that site was designed for cyclists like me. The women who have contacted me think being active means only going out for dinner!"

Finished with our refreshments, we pedal out of town on S. Rocky River Drive, which takes us past two attractive and well-maintained Victorian homes. They have kept their period look and it is easy to imagine a horse and buggy rolling up the drive.

We leave the horse-and-buggy scene in the background and continue until S. Rocky River Drive becomes Main Street. Shortly thereafter, we turn right onto Strongsville Boulevard, which soon takes us to Big Creek Parkway. We turn left and retrace our earlier path through Big Creek Reservation, enjoying the rest of the journey together.

Berea

Early in its settlement, Berea was called Lyceum Village, echoing Aristotle's Athenian garden. Its early settlers attempted to establish it as a Christian utopian community, but small membership in the group doomed it to failure, and it closed in 1844. In the meantime, however, a circuit-riding Methodist preacher, Rev. Henry O. Sheldon, had arrived in the Berea area. Finding the settlement started there, he became its first postmaster. In that position, it fell to him to give the place an official name. Being biblically inclined, Sheldon thought of two possibilities—Berea and Tabor. Since he had no strong preference, he made the choice with the flip of a coin. (We presume that since he was a preacher, he considered the choice guided by providence rather than luck.)

A New England transplant, John Baldwin, had more of an economic impact on the community when he invented a lathe to cut slabs of stone into grindstones, thus launching the sandstone mining industry along the banks of the river in the 1840s. That business continued for nearly a century until grindstones were superseded by carborundum grinding wheels and cement began to be widely used in construction. Baldwin also founded Baldwin Institute, a school that later merged with German Wallace College to become today's Baldwin Wallace College, in the heart of Berea. Today, Berea is also known as the home of the Cleveland Browns training facility.

Miles and Directions

Note: Mileage given is from the roadway. If you ride the trail, distances may be slightly different because trail winds a bit.

0.0	Exit Lower Fern Hill picnic area toward road and turn left onto Big Creek Parkway. If using trail, exit picnic area at end opposite from road. Cross footbridge at west end of picnic area and follow trail, taking right fork when it splits
0.9	Cross Snow Road
2.0	Cross Stumph Road
3.1	Cross W. 130th Street
3.7	Cross Smith Road
4.6	Cross Bagley Road
5.8	Cross Fowles Road
6.4	Cross Main Street
7.4	Turn right onto Valley Parkway
7.5	Turn left onto Whitney Road and cross covered bridge
7.8	At left bend, Whitney Road becomes Eastland Road
8.3	Turn right onto Fair Road (trail ends here)
9.9	Turn right onto Priem Road
10.0	Turn right onto W. Sprague Road
10.1	Turn left onto Fair Street
10.3	Turn right onto Meadow Drive
10.6	Jog right onto Prospect Street/SR237, then left onto S. Quarry Lane (trail resumes here)
10.8	Turn left onto Valley Parkway
11.5	Turn right onto N. Quarry Lane
11.8	Turn left onto S. Rocky River Drive
11.9	Turn left onto W. Bridge Street
	Café Ah-Roma on right
11.9	Turn left onto W. Bridge Street
12.0	Turn right onto S. Rocky River Drive
13.0	Cross Eastland Road. S. Rocky River Drive becomes Main Street
13.8	Turn right onto Strongsville Boulevard
14. 1	Turn left onto Big Creek Parkway and retrace route to starting point
20.8	Arrive at Lower Fern Hill picnic area

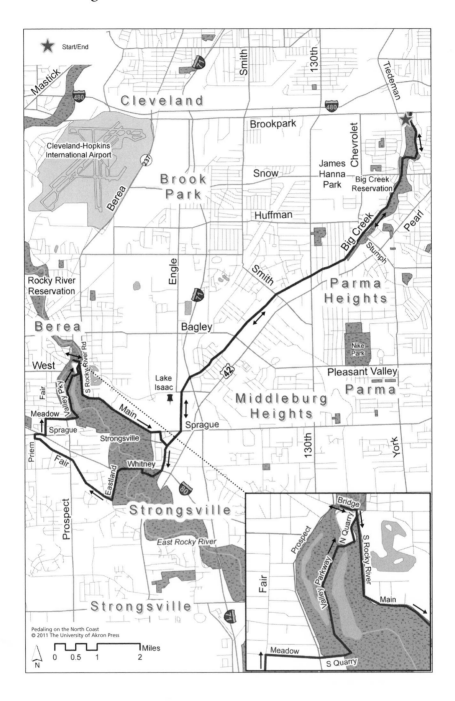

Ride 10
The Towpath

Route: The Ohio & Erie Towpath Trail within
Cuyahoga Valley National Park
Distance: Round-trip
Main Route: 27 miles, North Extension: 12 miles,
South Extension: 14 miles
Main Route + North Extension: 39 miles
Main Route + South Extension: 40 miles
Main Route + North and Sound Extensions: 52 miles
With train one way
Main Route 13 miles
Main Route + South Extension: 20 miles
Main Route + North and South Extensions: 32
No train service in North Extension
Terrain: Mostly flat
Communities Visited: *Main Route*—Independence,
Brecksville, Peninsula. *North Extension*—Valley View,
Cuyahoga Heights, Cleveland. *South Extension*—Boston
Township, Cuyahoga Falls

Starting/Ending Point: *Southbound on Main Route—* Rockside Road trailhead; *Southbound on North Extension—*W. Harvard Road trailhead; *Northbound on Main Route and North Extension—*Peninsula Trailhead; *Northbound on South Extension—*Botzum

Points of Interest: Towpath Trail, Canal Visitor Center, Ohio & Erie Canal, canal locks, Jaite Mill site, Boston Store Visitor Center, M. D. Garage (art exhibits), Peninsula Depot Visitor Center, Great Blue Heron rookery, Eagle nest

How to Get There: *To Rockside Trailhead—*Take I-77 to exit 155 (Rockside Road). Go east on Rockside. Just before the traffic light at Canal Road, turn right into the Lock 39/ Rockside Trailhead.

*To the Rockside Train Station—*Take I-77 to exit 155 (Rockside Road). Go east on Rockside. Turn left (north) on Canal Road and then left (west) on Old Rockside Road. Turn left into the Rockside Station parking lot.

*To the Peninsula Trailhead and Train Station—*Take I-77 to exit 145 (SR21). Take SR21 south to SR303. Take SR303 east to Peninsula. Turn left on N. Locust Street. Turn left on Mill Street. The train station is on Mill Street after one block, where the street bends to the right. The trailhead is at the first turn to the left after the bend.

*To Botzum Trailhead and Train Station—*Take I-77 to exit 145 (SR21). Take SR21 south to SR303. Take SR303 east to Riverview Road. Turn right on Riverview and continue about six miles. Turn right into Botzum trailhead and train station parking (Also called Indian Mound Trailhead).

Riding the Cuyahoga Valley Scenic Railroad

The train operates: weekends in April–May, Wednesdays through Sunday in June–October, and special events excursions by announcement.

For schedules, visit www.cvsr.com or call 1-800-468-4070.

As of 2010, cyclists and their bikes can ride the train in one direction for as far as it goes for only $2. (For adult non-cyclists, a ride-all-day ticket is $15).

Cleveland's river is the Cuyahoga, which winds from Geauga County, through Akron, and up to Lake Erie, just west of downtown (the Lake Parks West ride begins at the mouth). The meeting of river and lake was a primary reason that, in 1796, Moses Cleaveland selected the surrounding land to establish the settlement that he expected to become the "capital city" of the Connecticut Western Reserve—what we know today as Cleveland.

On its way to the lake, the Cuyahoga runs through a valley of lush beauty, much of which has been reclaimed or kept from development and is now preserved as the Cuyahoga Valley National Park.

The park runs from the Cleveland suburb of Independence south to the city of Cuyahoga Falls. Additionally, it connects with Cleveland's substantial Metroparks system to the east, west and north. At its southern boundary, it links with other parks and corridors of green space that extend all the way to New Phil-

---

The Cuyahoga River

On a map of Ohio, the Cuyahoga River forms a giant "U," rising from two springs in Ohio's Geauga County, in the adjacent townships of Hambden and Montville. The Hambden stream becomes the west branch of the Cuyahoga; the Montville stream, the east branch. The two, flowing south, merge in Burton Township and continue south as (in the nomenclature of the watershed district) the "upper" Cuyahoga River, through the tiny community of Hiram Rapids and then southwest through Mantua, Kent, and Munroe Falls. It then meanders westward as the "middle" Cuyahoga River, through Cuyahoga Falls and into Akron, where it swings approximately north-northwest and travels through the Cuyahoga Valley National Park. It emerges from the park and continues northward toward Lake Erie as the "lower" Cuyahoga River. The sources and mouth of the river are about thirty-five miles apart, but the river is ninety miles long.

Before arriving at the lake, the river divides the east and west sides of Cleveland. Before 1827, the last bend of the river channeled the water to its mouth about a mile farther west than it is today. But in 1827, the present mouth was dug, severing the Whiskey Island peninsula at it east end from the mainland (see Lake Parks West ride) and creating a more direct channel to Lake Erie.

Cleveland's early business district was right on the river, serviced by river, lake and canal boats. Eventually, industry took over most of the riverfront property.

Changing Gears

Thanks to the efforts of local citizens' associations and the legislative work of the late Congressman John F. Seiberling, Congressman Ralph Regula, and the late Republican National Committee Chairman Ray Bliss, a large section of the Cuyahoga Valley has been reclaimed from settlement and development, and is now preserved as the Cuyahoga Valley National Park for everyone to enjoy.

adelphia, Ohio. All of these parks and corridors, along with the CVNP and portions of Greater Cleveland surrounding the river, are collectively referred to as the Ohio & Erie National Heritage Canalway.

Construction on the Ohio & Erie Canal, connecting Lake Erie at Cleveland to the Ohio River at Portsmouth, began in the 1820s and was completed in 1832. It helped to open up the Ohio frontier and provided the settlers with a reliable way to ship agricultural products and manufactured goods. While much of that canal no longer exists, its route is the backbone for the Canalway.

The Ohio & Erie Towpath Trail—"the Towpath," as it's commonly called—is an extensive recreational trail begun in the late twentieth century. It is planned to run 101 miles, from Cleveland to New Philadelphia, and nearly 90 percent of the Towpath is complete and rideable now, including the entire section of trail within the CVNP.

This ride offers a unique option: splitting the ride between train and bicycle. That is, you have an opportunity to ride the Cuyahoga Valley Scenic Railroad (CVSR) one way and pedal the other. The CVSR parallels the Cuyahoga River and Towpath and consists of a vintage passenger train that runs excursions north and south through the park. For cyclists, it's a great deal. As of this writing, cyclists can take the train with their bikes in one direction for as far as it goes for only $2.

We have designed this ride with three "modules," which, combined with the train option, means rides of several different lengths are possible:

Main Route: The Towpath Trail between Old Rockside Road and Peninsula is the Main Route and is the middle module. If you are not using the train one way, the Main Route round-trip ride is twenty-seven miles, which many riders will consider just right for a ride.

South Extension: The southern module, between Peninsula and Botzum is the South Extension. By itself, it is a round-trip of about fourteen miles (or only seven miles if you ride the train one way). If you ride the Main Route plus the South Extension, you will have pedaled almost the entire length of the CVNP.

North Extension: The northern module is the North Extension. While it is on the continuation of the Towpath, it leaves the CVNP and is in the Ohio & Erie Canal Reservation of the Cleveland Metroparks. There is no train service in the North Extension, so if you choose to ride it, you should plan to pedal that part both directions, a twelve-mile round-trip.

Our ride on the Towpath is on a chilly morning in September. Murray, Scott and I meet at the Rockside Depot of the CVSR, the northernmost point served by the excursion train. We intend to ride the rail to the southernmost depot within the park, Botzum, named for an early settler who farmed in that part of the Cuyahoga Valley. Using the nomenclature Murray and I established for this ride, our bicycle journey from Botzum back to Rockside will consist of the South Extension + Main Route, about twenty miles.

Train side, a railroad employee loads our bikes into a freight car while we board a passenger car designated for cyclists. The car is about a third full, and the train begins to move with surprising ease. It picks up speed and, by looking at the passing

---

The Ohio & Erie National Heritage Canalway

The parks, green corridors and communities along the northern third of the Ohio & Erie Canal are collectively referred to as the Ohio & Erie National Heritage Canalway. The Canalway is a region designated by Congress as a National Heritage Area "to help preserve and celebrate the rails, trails, landscapes, towns and sites that grew up along the first 110 miles of the canal that helped Ohio and our nation grow." Through the Canalway, the Cuyahoga Valley National Park is geographically linked to forty Ohio communities.

From www.ohioanderiecanalway.com

scenery of trees, river and meadows, we estimate that it holds a steady pace of no more than about 35 MPH.

The gentle rocking of the car gives us a pleasant sense of movement, and we chat quietly as the train continues down a corridor of natural beauty.

The train is powered by an old diesel engine, but as we pass a railroad maintenance yard on the right, the conductor tells us to look for the steam engine. One weekend a year, the Nickel Plate Road 14-wheel Berkshire No. 765 comes to pull the CVSR's train as a special event. The engine, owned by the Fort Wayne Railroad Historical Society, is the largest operating steam locomotive east of the Mississippi. That event is set for the next weekend, and the engine is already on site. We see it in all of its yesteryear splendor as we roll past.

During the summer, the train continues as far south as Canton, but now, after Labor Day, it turns around in Akron. Counting Rockside, there are seven stops within the park, with Botzum as the last. By the time we arrive at Botzum, slightly less than an hour after boarding, the car is comfortably full of riders. The Botzum station, like the others within the park, is a covered shelter where passengers can wait for the train, with the Towpath running nearby.

Just about everyone in the cyclist car gets off with us here. A train worker hands our bikes down from the freight car and, as we mount up, the train pulls away from the station.

We ride down the short connector path and turn north on the trail. Though the air-temperature is still cool, the mistiness has dissipated and the sun is shining. The wooded Towpath makes for nice shade.

Over most of its length, the Towpath's surface is finely crushed limestone. While not quite as easy to roll on as asphalt, it is nonetheless a reasonable hard-pack topping for a bicycle path. The main drawback about the Towpath is that, unless the trail is damp, your bike can end up covered in a coating of limestone dust. I discover this the first time I reach down for my water bottle and find the bottle, including the spout, covered with dust (note to self: on the Towpath, keep water bottle in bike trunk bag).

The towpath was constructed originally for horses and mules to trudge on as they pulled canal boats, so it's only natural that the current Towpath is right beside the remains of the canal. In some places, the only sign of the old canal is a wide extended ditch in which trees and other forest flora are growing. In other places, the canal bed is not visible at all, refilled and farmed over at some point after its closing. In still other sections, the canal is a water-filled channel, probably looking much as it did in its hey-day. At various spots along the way, we pass the stone remnants of the original locks, though none of these are operational now.

Being a canal path, the Towpath has very little rise and fall and we seldom have to shift gears as we ride. That flatness is one of the factors, along with the natural beauty and sense of history the Towpath embodies, that makes the trail so popular with recreational cyclists. It's not uncommon to come upon whole families, including young children, mounted on bikes or walking the path.

Today is a weekday and the trail is not overly crowded, although there are still a substantial number of people, both on foot and on wheels. We're headed north and, periodically, we pass other northbound trail users and meet southbounders. But there's no sense of rush; everyone is courteous about making room for overtaking and oncoming traffic.

Although often hidden by the trees, we see the river from time to time as it snakes along near the trail, sometimes to our right and sometimes to our left. If you were canoeing through the park on the river, your journey would be considerably longer than the Towpath, because of the wriggling track of the water-way. In fact, Cuyahoga means "crooked," and that accurately describes this river. The Cuyahoga rises just thirty miles south of its mouth at Lake Erie, but is ninety miles long, and about twen-ty-two of those miles are in the CVNP.

Within the park, the only dining opportunities convenient to the Towpath are in Peninsula and at Rockside Road. After only slightly less than seven miles of riding, we pass the Peninsula trail-head, but none of us are ready to eat, so we opt to wait for Rockside.

Peninsula is a quaint and charming village, and it's worth getting off the trail to explore it, whether you're planning on eating there or not. During the canal era, Peninsula had a seaport-like atmosphere, complete with hotels and saloons. Today, it's a quiet hamlet replete with nineteenth-century architecture, offering shops and galleries for the pleasure of park visitors. There's also a bicycle shop in Peninsula—Century Cycles—where you can rent a bike to ride in the park, get repairs, or stock up on gear (for more on Peninsula, see the Western Reserve Ramble ride).

The next trailhead we come to is where the Towpath crosses Boston Mills Road. In the canal era, the village at this location, Boston, specialized in building and repairing canal boats. (The Boston-to-Bedford Bikeabout ride starts at this location.)

Before we come to the next trailhead, the one at Highland/Vaughn Road, we pass on our left the site of the old Jaite Paper Mill. The mill closed in 1951 and burned down in the 1980s. What remains on the site today is a large rusting Fourdrinier paper machine, a massive assembly of gears and rollers that looks something like a large printing press. It was left on the site as part of an outdoor exhibit. Shortly after we cross Highland/Vaughn Road, we look left and see several wooden buildings, all painted an identical yellow. These are left over from the Jaite company town that was once here. Today, they serve as the headquarters of the CVNP.

The rows of yellow houses trigger a memory for Scott. Between college and grad school, he says, he worked reading meters for the

Dining Along the Towpath Trail

Peninsula

Fisher's Café and Pub
1607 Main Street
(330) 657-2651
Sandwiches, salads,
and specialty meals

Winking Lizard Tavern
1615 Main Street
(330) 467-1002
Sandwiches, salads,
and specialty meals

Thornburg Station, Old Rockside Road

Yours Truly
8111 Rockside Road #102
(216) 524-8111
Wide menu of breakfast,
lunch, and dinner foods

Lockkeeper's Inn
8001 Rockside Road
(216) 524-9404
Specialty Italian dishes,
pizza, and sandwiches

Kentucky Power Company. One of his routes was in Wheelwright, another company town—in that case a coal-mining company. By the time Scott read meters there, the houses were privately owned and had been personalized by their owners, but he remembered them as all being architecturally identical.

We continue on the trail and eventually pass under a high bridge that carries SR82. A section of the trail in this area is blacktopped. Murray explains that some of that is because seasonal flooding in this area would wash out an unpaved trail, while some is because paved sections were added to allow farmers

> **Changing Gears**
>
> Rail lines were first laid through the valley in 1873. The greater efficiency of the trains, which drove development in the region, eventually doomed the canal. The canal continued to operate for a time after the railroad came, but following a massive flood in 1913, it was abandoned.

access to lands still under cultivation when some parts of the area were transitioning from private to park lands. These farms have now reverted to woodlands. Just north of the high bridge, Murray tells us to look left, across the river at a stand of dead trees, killed off by flooding around them. High in the branches of several of these trees are large nests, which Murray says are built by blue herons. The entire area is, in fact, a blue heron rookery. In addition, we spot a larger nest belonging to a pair of eagles, who, says Murray, have produced an eaglet this year.

About halfway between Highland/Vaughn Road and the next one north, Pleasant Valley/Alexander Road, the Towpath emerges from the woods. It still runs beside the canal, but now, immediately across the canal on our right is Canal Road. There's a bridge over the canal at this point that allows us to leave the trail and cross the road to visit the Frazee House. This Federal style home was built in 1826 by settler Stephen Frazee, making it one of the oldest brick homes in the valley. It is normally open to the public, so we ride over to check it out. However, we find it temporarily closed for "structure stabilization." While we are slightly disappointed, it is good to see that preservation work continues in the park. Several of the old locks on the Towpath also seemed to be undergoing preservative efforts.

Returning to the Trail, we continue to the Hillside Road trailhead. Here an old canal-era building serves as the Canal Visitor Center. Inside, it has displays that explain how the canal was built and how the locks operated.

A final two-mile stretch on the Towpath brings us to Rockside Road, which the Towpath goes under via a tunnel. We continue through the tunnel, completing our run a few hundred yards on the north side, at Old Rockside road. There, immediately beside the Trail, is Thornburg Station, a commercial complex with two restaurants, a candy store, office space and parking. We stop at Yours Truly for lunch.

The Yours Truly menu is extensive. Scott has a bowl of chili and a chicken-walnut salad sandwich combo, Murray has blueberry pancakes, I have a veggie quesadilla, and we all pronounce our meals as an excellent conclusion to a great ride.

The Canal Locks

The Ohio & Erie Canal—Cleveland to Portsmouth, Ohio—was 308 miles long, with 146 lift locks, and a total rise of 1,206 feet. The highest point was the Portage summit, between Akron and Barberton. From there to Lake Erie, the canal stepped downward by means of forty-four lift locks, which enabled canal boats to rise and drop with terrain. The locks on the canal were chambers of quarried limestone with gates on each end. By releasing and admitting water into the chamber, each lock was capable of lifting and lowering boats about eight feet. Remains of several locks are visible along the Towpath Trail today and remnants of more can be seen in other places throughout the Ohio & Erie National Heritage Canalway.

Miles and Directions

Southbound
North Extension: W. Harvard Road trailhead to Old Rockside Road is 5.9 miles. (No train service in North Extension)

0.0	Enter Towpath Trail at Old Rockside Road, heading south or from Rockside/Lock 39 Trailhead, heading south
2.0	Cross Hillside Road; continue on Towpath Trail
3.8	Frazee House
6.4	Cross under Chippewa Road Bridge; continue on Towpath Trail
6.6	Station Road Bridge
9.2	Cross Highland Road; continue on Towpath Trail
9.6	Jaite Mill site
11.1	Cross Boston Mills Road; continue on Towpath Trail
13.4	Arrive Peninsula Towpath Trail parking lot; exit parking lot, cross railroad tracks and turn left onto West Mill Street
13.6	Turn right onto North Locust Street
13.7	Turn right onto Main Street/SR303
13.7	Lunch, Fisher's Café and Pub or The Winking Lizard
13.7	Retrace route to start point or ride train back
27.4	Arrive at Old Rockside Road or at Rockside/Lock 39 trailhead

South Extension: Peninsula to Botzum is 6.8 miles.

Northbound
South Extension: Botzum to Peninsula is 6.8 miles.

0.0	Enter Towpath Trail at Peninsula trailhead, heading north
2.3	Cross Boston Mills Road; continue on Towpath Trail
3.8	Jaite Mill site
4.2	Cross Highland Road; continue on Towpath Trail
6.8	Station Road Bridge
7.0	Cross under Chippewa Road Bridge; continue on Towpath Trail
9.6	Frazee House

11.4   Cross Hillside Road; continue on Towpath Trail

13.2   Path to Rockside/Lock 39 Trailhead. Proceed through tunnel under Rockside Road

13.4   Arrive at Old Rockside Road

13.4   Lunch, Yours Truly and Lockkeeper's Inn are beside trail at Old Rockside Road

13.4   Retrace route to start point or ride train back

26.8   Arrive at Peninsula trailhead

North Extension: Old Rockside to Road W. Harvard Road trailhead is 5.9 miles. (No train service in North Extension)

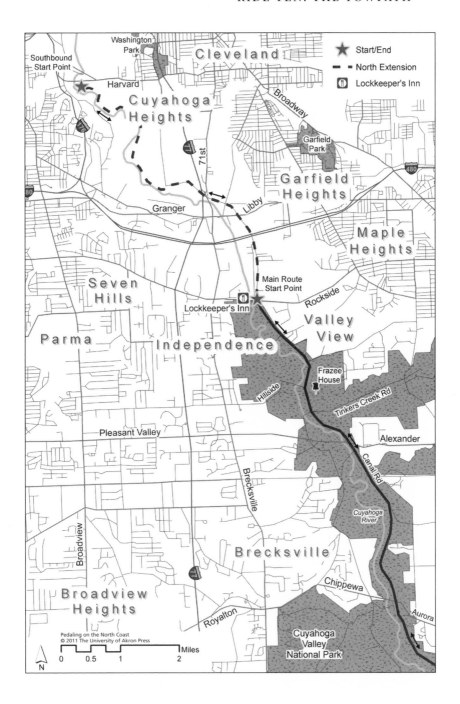

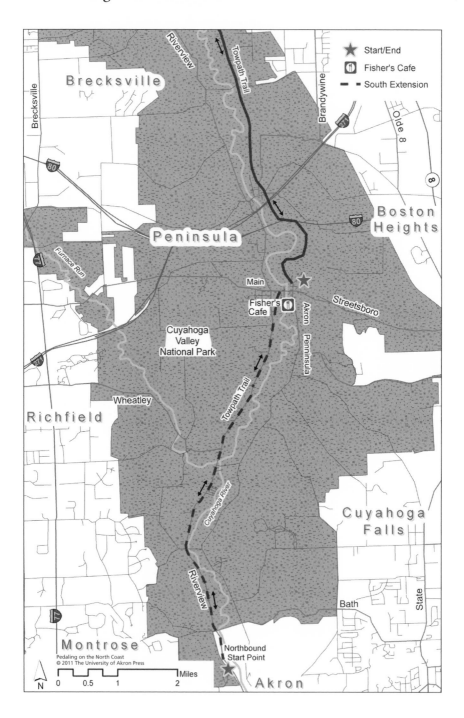

Start/End

Fisher's Cafe

South Extension

Brecksville

Brecksville

Riverview

Towpath Trail

Brandywine

Olde 8

80

8

Boston
Heights

80

Furnace Run

Peninsula

Main

Streetsboro

Fisher's
Cafe

Akron Peninsula

Cuyahoga
Valley
National Park

Wheatley

Richfield

Towpath Trail

Cuyahoga River

Cuyahoga
Falls

Riverview

Bath

State

Montrose

Northbound
Start Point

Akron

Pedaling on the North Coast
© 2011 The University of Akron Press

N

Miles
0   0.5   1   2

The Cleveland skyline at night. *Courtesy of David Ploenzke*

Lakewood Police Department Bicycle Brigade in 1914. Motorcycles replaced bicycles from 1925 until the 1990s, when the bicycle patrols resumed. *Courtesy of the Cleveland Memory Project*

Detail of the Soldiers and Sailors Monument in Public Square. The monument, designed by Levi Scofield, opened in 1894 and is dedicated to Civil War soldiers and sailors from Cuyahoga County. *Courtesy of Thomas Bacher*

An early postcard of the beach at Euclid Beach Park. The park, built around the beach, was open from 1895–1969 and featured roller coasters, a carousel, athletics, and other attractions. *Courtesy of the Cleveland Memory Project*

The Cleveland Museum of Art, as seen from across Wade Lagoon. Opened in 1916, the museum has a renowned collection of over thirty thousand works. *Courtesy of the Cleveland Museum of Art*

Mural celebrating Italian heritage in Cleveland's Little Italy, a neighborhood with a rich history and selection of restaurants, bakeries, and art galleries. The neighborhood hosts an annual Feast of the Assumption Festival every August. *Courtesy of David Ploenzke*

The main building of the Cleveland Botanical Garden. Founded in 1930, the garden is open year-round and houses twenty specialty gardens and indoor biomes with a diverse selection of plant and animal life. *Courtesy of the Cleveland Botanical Garden*

The waterfall on the Chagrin River in the village of Chagrin Falls. Incorporated in 1844, Chagrin Falls is a village of just over four thousand people, with many shops and restaurants. *Courtesy of B. Katz*

The Shakespeare (or British) Garden in the Cleveland Cultural Gardens. Founded in 1916, the cultural gardens comprise over seventy acres and thirty individual gardens, representing cultures from all over the world. *Courtesy of the Cleveland Public Library*

The Leonard Krieger CanalWay Center offers indoor exhibits and programming focused on the relationships between people, nature, and industry, while also serving as a visitor center and gift shop along the Towpath Trail. *Courtesy of Casey Batule & Cleveland Metroparks*

The Rainforest at the Cleveland Metroparks Zoo. Opened in 1882, the zoo features several different exhibits, notably the Rainforest—a large indoor tropical environment with many different animals and plants. *Courtesy of the Cleveland Metroparks Zoo*

Built in the 1890s as the gatehouse to Feargus Squire's proposed mansion, Squire's Castle is all that remains of the never-completed project. The castle has been a part of the Cleveland Metroparks since 1925, and it remains open to the public and a popular picnic spot. *Courtesy of the Cleveland Memory Project*

Inside the West Side Market. First the site of an open air market in 1840, the current market-house was erected in 1912. Featuring over one hundred ethnically diverse vendors, the market offers a variety of vegetables, dairy, meats, seafood, and specialty foods. *Courtesy of Curt Brown*

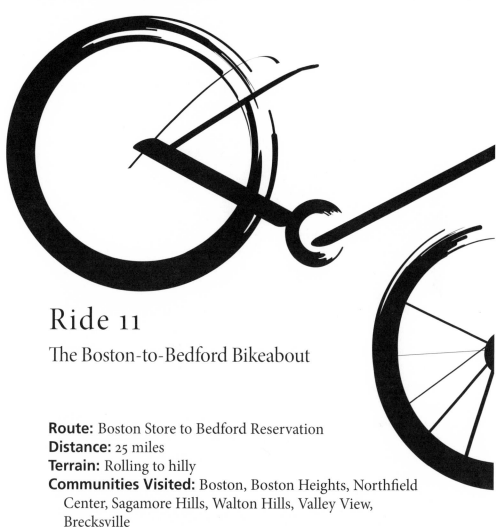

Ride 11

The Boston-to-Bedford Bikeabout

Route: Boston Store to Bedford Reservation
Distance: 25 miles
Terrain: Rolling to hilly
Communities Visited: Boston, Boston Heights, Northfield Center, Sagamore Hills, Walton Hills, Valley View, Brecksville
Starting/Ending Point: Boston Store Visitor Center
Points of Interest: Boston Store Visitor Center, Boston general Store, Cuyahoga Valley National Park, Bike & Hike Trail, Brandywine Falls, Bedford Reservation, Ohio and Erie Canal, Jaite, Boston Mills Ski Resort
How to Get There: Take I-77 to exit 146 (I-80/Ohio Turnpike/SR21). Turn right (south) on SR21. Turn left (east) on Boston Mills Road. Cross Riverview Road and railroad tracks and then turn right into Boston Store Visitor Center.

In Murray's introduction, he mentions that he and I count hills differently. He counts them if there's even a half-percent grade while I, he says, count them only if I have to use my granny gear. Despite our differences, for this ride we agree: there are seven hills.

Murray and I also agree that only one of these hills is "really" big, but if you ride this circuit counter-clockwise (as we do), you will encounter it right away on the south end of the course. If you'd rather defer climbing for a bit, you can pedal the circuit clockwise, ascend a different hill at the north end (at about the midpoint of the ride), and finish on a long downslope. Either way, you have to climb out of the valley once, and you get to sail back down into it once.

We tackle the ride on a hot afternoon in early August, starting in the Cuyahoga Valley National Park at the Boston Store Visitor Center (for more on the CVNP, see the Towpath ride). The land surrounding the visitor center was once the village of Boston, though you may hear it referred to as "Boston Mills," the name of both a road and of the nearby depot of the Cuyahoga Valley Scenic Railroad. In the 1900s, the "Mills" referred to the paper mill and flour mills that were located nearby. Today, in addition to being a street and depot, it's the name of a popular ski resort there.

The village of Boston was established in 1806, but it was the opening of the Ohio & Erie Canal through the hamlet in 1827 that brought the first building boom. The canal gave the community its main industry; constructing and repairing canal boats. To handle this, the villagers built dry docks, and eventually a water-powered mill, a warehouse, two stores, a hotel and some other enterprises.

Changing Gears

The 1836 Boston Company Store, with its Federal and Greek Revival architecture, now serves as a Cuyahoga Valley National Park visitor center, with a small bookstore and exhibits about the construction of canal boats. The Towpath is immediately beside it, and many trail users and other park visitors enjoy a rest on the store's long veranda.

The arrival of the Valley Railway in 1880 began the decline of the canal, but the trains brought another growth period to the village. The railroad made it easy to ship products, and the Cleveland-Akron Bag Company set up shop in Boston in 1899. The company built six houses, two duplexes, and a company store to accommodate the new residents who came to Boston to work in the factory. The flood of 1913 finished off the canal, and the bag company closed ten years later due to lack of sufficient water to operate.

The village no longer exists and the canal channel is dry, but a few buildings from various eras of the community's history remain. The old store, built in 1836, is now the visitor center and houses displays about canal boat construction. It's worth your time to view the displays at the start or end of your ride.

Murray and I head out of the Visitor Center parking lot and turn right onto Boston Mills Road. Within just a few strokes of the pedals, we come to a Y fork in the road. To our left is Hines Hill Road. On our right is the continuation of Boston Mills. They both go up the big hill, reaching the top about a mile apart. Following our planned route, we stay on Boston Mills Road and start climbing. Partway up the hill, I look down to a wooded ravine on my right and spot a large buck. I've seen does and fawns in the park before, but this is the first time I've spotted an adult male. It seems that the park always has something new to offer. He stares at me, seemingly unconcerned, and I continue my upward trek.

Boston

In the boom time of the canal, Boston, with its canal-boat-building industry, was thriving. The *Allen Trimble*, one of maiden boats on the canal, was constructed in Boston and launched on June 3, 1827 as part of a flotilla that celebrated the canal opening.

Later in the same century, Boston was home to John Brown, the leader of a gang of counterfeiters (not the famed abolitionist). He was eventually arrested and acquitted, and then became Boston's justice of the peace.

All that remains of Boston today are a few old buildings preserved to give the flavor of the period. The old Boston Store, right beside the Towpath, is a museum about canal-boat construction. Just west of the store is the M.D. Garage, a Pure Oil Company gas station, preserved with its 1940s look. No gasoline is sold there today, but the station periodically houses art shows. Directly across the street from the garage is another store, dating from about 1900; named Trail Mix, it's a snack stop for park visitors.

After climbing for almost a mile, the road descends a little and then levels out. I am just settling into a nice cruise, however, when it bounds upward again, eventually reaching the real top, in rural Boston Heights. This community was originally part of Boston, but broke away in 1924 to become its own Summit County village.

A bit farther on, I come to Bike & Hike Trail as it crosses Boston Mills Road. The Bike & Hike is part of our route, so I dismount and wait for Murray, who is not far behind. The thermometer on my bike registers 85 degrees, and I am glad for the opportunity to cool down.

The Bike & Hike Trail was one of the first "rails to trails" conversions in the country, laid out on the course of the old Akron, Bedford & Cleveland Railroad, known commonly as "the ABC." Built in 1895, the ABC was the longest electric railroad of its kind at the time. Riders could take it from Akron to Cleveland's Public Square for fifty cents, making the trip in about two and a half hours. The service ended in 1932. Today, 33.5 miles of the rail route has been converted to trail, and all of it is paved. The trail is a facility of the Metro Parks, serving Summit County, and it is a great gift to the area. We're using only the northern eight miles of it today.

Murray rolls to a stop beside me. "We might have picked a cooler day," he comments, but then he grins, and I know he's having as much fun as I am being outdoors on a sunny Ohio day, surrounded by the high green of summer.

Rested now, and with the big hill behind us, we turn north on the trail and start rolling through a shady, tree-lined green corridor. There are a few other riders and some walkers on the trail and we glide along easily, conversing as we proceed.

Eventually the trail emerges onto Brandywine Road. Here the old rail line no longer exists, removed by the construction of the I-271 highway. So, for the next mile, the trail joins Brandywine Road. Since the road is not heavily traveled, the deviation from the rail path is not a problem, though there is a dip down and then back up on the roadway. (In case you're counting, the "back up" part is the second hill.) The reward for being on the road, however, is that it takes us by the entrance to Brandywine Falls, which, at seventy-five feet, is one of the highest waterfalls in Ohio. We can't see the falls from the road, but by turning in at the short entrance road just after we cross the bridge over I-271, we come to a boardwalk, which we follow on foot to the viewing area that overlooks the falls. The falls are beautiful, and definitely worth stopping to see.

Back on our bikes, we continue a little farther on Brandywine Road to where the Bike & Hike trail resumes, and we turn onto it. The whole time we have been on the trail and Brandywine Road, we were right on the eastern boundary of the CVNP, but about a mile and a half after the trail resumes, somewhere between its crossing of Boyden and Holzhauer Roads, we leave the parklands behind, though the trail continues through a broad strip of natural foliage. Jurisdictionally, we have moved from Boston Heights to Northfield Center to Sagamore Hills, all within Summit County.

We now come to a new element on the trail: high-voltage electric transmission towers. In some places, these towers are right beside the trail and in others, they straddle it. Their steel skeletons are a dominant feature on the continuing route of the trail, but they don't distract from the beautiful ride. As we re-enter the trail after crossing Aurora Road/SR82, a sign beside the entrance tells us that the trail in this area is provided "in cooperation with First Energy," an area power company.

Being on a rail bed, the trail has very little rise and fall, with high ground cut down to grade and low ground filled up to grade. The latter is especially apparent after we cross Sagamore Road. The natural terrain is a deep ravine, but the trail traverses it on a high bank, originally built for the trains. The land falls away quickly on both sides of the trail.

When we crossed Sagamore Road, we entered Cuyahoga County, and the community of Walton Hills. While the Bike & Hike ends at the Alexander Road Trailhead, another paved trail takes over directly across Alexander. This is a Cleveland

Metroparks multi-use path. We follow it as it turns east immediately, running beside Alexander Road to the next intersection, which is Dunham Road. As we turn left with the trail beside Dunham, we enter the Bedford Reservation of the Cleveland Metroparks. Staying on the trail, we turn with it beside Egbert Road and a bit farther on, we turn left with the trail onto Overlook Lane. The stretch from where we entered Egbert to where we entered Overlook Lane is all up hill, the third climb of the ride.

Overlook Lane ends at Gorge Parkway; here Bedford Reservation has a beautiful gorge through which Tinkers Creek flows as it heads for union with the Cuyahoga River. The creek snakes westward through the reservation at the bottom of the chasm. Gorge Parkway runs on the top and then plunges down to the creek level.

The multi-use trail we are on turns east to continue beside the parkway. Our route goes west, but Murray suggests we first go just a short distance east to a viewing area that overlooks the deep valley and the creek. We do, and the view is stunning, a panorama of forested gorge with the creek at the bottom. Murray tells me that I should come back in the autumn when the leaves are turning colors. That, he says, makes the view even more breathtaking.

After a good look, we wheel out onto Gorge Parkway and head west. Shortly after we pass the Overlook Lane junction, we find ourselves on a mile-long downhill romp. Because of the trees and vegetation, we cannot always see the creek as we plummet down the gorge, although as we near the bottom, we are rolling right beside it.

Gorge Parkway ends at Dunham Road. We turn right, cross the creek on a bridge and then turn left onto Tinkers Creek Road. A roadside sign tells us we are leaving Walton Hills. A short distance farther, another sign informs us we are entering Valley View. We ride onto Tinkers Creek Road and find houses on both sides; we are not on parkway any longer.

Before proceeding far on this road, however, we come to our lunch stop on the left, Tinkers Creek Road Tavern. The tav-

ern sits beside the creek with both indoor seating and a patio next to the water. The lunch menu
is impressive, and the evening menu offers full
meals. Murray has the Tavern Burger with the
signature homemade potato chips. I have a black-
ened grouper sandwich and fries.

Changing Gears

Tinkers Creek Road Tavern
14000 Tinkers Creek Road
(216) 642-3900
Sandwiches, meals

After lunch, we continue west on Tinkers Creek Road, which
is flat and not heavily traveled, making it an easy passage.

Eventually Tinkers Creek Road tees into Canal Road, on which
we turn south, re-entering the national park. As its name suggests,
Canal Road is right beside the old Ohio & Erie Canal. Farther
south, much of the canal bed is a dry trench filled with vegetation
or obliterated by later land use, but here, the canal is filled with
water. The Towpath Trail (see Towpath ride) is on its west bank
and Canal Road on its east bank. Almost immediately, we cross
a bridge that spans the creek. Tinkers Creek flows not only under
the road at this point, but also under pipes bridging the canal water
above the creek so the creek can flow unhindered to the Cuyahoga
River, which is just west of the canal. In its operating era, the canal
crossed above the creek in a channel-wide aqueduct. Murray tells
me that the pipes are soon to be replaced with an aqueduct again,
restoring historical authenticity to this section of the canal.

Continuing south on Canal Road, we soon come to an exit
ramp on the left that takes us up to where Alexander/Pleasant
Valley Road crosses above Canal Road, the canal and Towpath,

Tinkers Creek Road Tavern

The building housing Tinkers Creek Road Tavern has a colorful history. It was built as a home in 1902, but soon became a beer garden. The liquor license for that establishment is one of the oldest on
record in the state of Ohio. For many years, the tavern had a reputation as a "run-down place," lacking windows and having few operating lights. It was dark, smoke-filled, and some said it had a notice-
able odor. The basement has bullet holes where patrons gathered
for drinks and target practice. The current owners stripped the building to the studs and started over, adding plenty of windows and the
patio in the process, and making it a place working to earn a new
reputation as an excellent eatery.

the river, and the rail line used by the Cuyahoga Valley Scenic Railroad. At the top of the ramp, we turn right onto Pleasant Valley Road. Once across all those arteries, we make two quick lefts that put us onto Riverview Road, at its northern terminus.

From this point, Riverview Road runs southward paralleling the river not only to Boston, but continuing through the CVNP and on into Cuyahoga Falls. To say it parallels the river, however, is not to say that it is on its bank. For most of the way to Boston, we cannot even see the river, due sometimes to the forestation and sometimes to the river's wandering course. The rail line, which is between the road and the river, is visible from the road more often, but not the whole way.

What's more, the road does not stay on the valley floor. Sometimes it crawls over the hips of hills running transversely into the valley. Murray and I count four hills between the north end of Riverview Road and Boston. None of these, however, is on the scale of the Boston Mills Road hill. The first of these four, which we encounter soon after embarking on Riverview, is fairly steep, but mercifully short. The rest are longer, but not as steep.

The northernmost section of Riverview is within the national park boundaries. We pass some pastureland and then woods, climbing the next hill.

At some point, we enter the environs of the city of Brecksville, and Riverview becomes a residential road. When we cross Chippewa Road/SR82, Riverview plunges quickly downhill and back into the park, where it remains the rest of the way to Boston.

The road proceeds through woods and by fields, climbing over the last two of the hills and past a couple of small farmsteads, holdovers from the pre-park days. Now, however, the park owns the farms, and families run them using sustainable agriculture practices and per park guidelines.

At the intersection with Vaughn Road are several wooden buildings, all painted an identical yellow. These are the remains of Jaite, which we explore further in the Towpath ride. Once a company town, the buildings now house the headquarters and various functions of the National Park service.

Continuing, Riverview Road at last brings us down to the valley floor. Soon, looming on our right is the Boston Mills Ski Resort. Being midsummer, the slopes are quiet as we pass.

Across the street from the resort is a small station of the Cuyahoga Valley Scenic Railroad, the Boston Mills stop. Just beyond the station, we come to Boston Mills Road. Murray and I turn left and roll into Boston, concluding this ride where we started, at the Boston Store Visitor Center.

Boston Mills Ski Resort

This seventy-nine-acre resort offers both beginner and advance slopes, including the steepest ski slope in Ohio. With a large clubhouse and food service, it hosts many patrons in cold weather.

The resort also features one summer event, a fine-arts show, held each year on the two weekends around July 4. The event showcases the work of local and regional artists and artisans, and includes live music and food vendors.

Miles and Directions

0.0	Leave Boston Store Visitor Center, heading east (right) on Boston Mills Road
0.1	Take right fork, staying on Boston Mills Road
2.4	Turn left onto Bike and Hike Trail
3.8	Turn left onto Brandywine Road
4.3	Cross entrance to Brandywine Falls
4.8	Turn left onto Bike and Hike Trail
5.8	Cross S. Boyden Road; jog slightly left to continue on trail
7.3	Cross Aurora Road (SR82). CAUTION
10.4	Cross Alexander Road; follow trail as it turns right
10.7	Turn left onto Dunham Road
11.1	Turn right onto Egbert Road
11.3	Turn left onto Overlook Lane
12.2	Turn left onto Gorge Parkway (To visit the gorge overlook, turn right about a quarter mile. The overlook is on the left. Then return to the Overlook Lane junction and continue west on Gorge Parkway)
13.3	Turn right onto Dunham Road
13.4	Turn left onto Tinkers Creek Road
15.1	Turn left onto Canal Road
16.0	Exit Canal Road by exit ramp on left, up to Pleasant Valley Road/Alexander Road
16.1	Turn right onto Pleasant Valley Road
16.7	Turn left onto Brookside Road
16.8	Turn left onto Riverview Road
19.8	Cross Chippewa Road (SR82)
22.6	Cross Vaughn Road
24.5	Turn left onto Boston Mills Road
24.7	Turn right into Boston Store Visitor Center

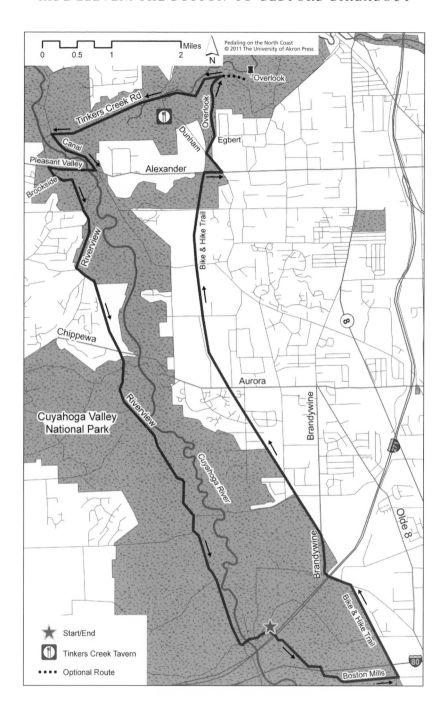

Ride 12
Chagrin Falls Meander

Route: Sagamore Hills to Chagrin Falls
Distance: 40 miles
Terrain: Mostly flat. One hill and some rolling sections
Communities Visited: Sagamore Hills, Walton Hills,
  Bedford, Bedford Heights, Oakwood, Glenwillow, Solon,
  Bentleyville, Chagrin Falls, Reminderville, Twinsburg,
  Macedonia, Northfield Center Boston Store Visitor Center
Starting/Ending Point: Sagamore Square shopping
  center (Marc's is the main store), 550 West Aurora Road,
  Northfield, OH 44067-2108
Points of Interest: The Emerald Necklace, Chagrin Falls
  Village, the falls
How to Get There: Take I-77 to exit 149. Go east on
  Royalton Road/SR82, which becomes Chippewa Road/SR82,
  which becomes W. Aurora Road/SR82. Sagamore Square
  shopping center is at 550 W. Aurora Road, on the southeast
  corner where Holzhauer Road tees into SR82 from the
  south.

T his sweeping loop travels through or along the edge of thirteen communities of the Greater Cleveland and northern Summit County area, but aside from Chagrin Falls (where you can stop for lunch), there's little sense of riding through towns. The outbound ride is almost entirely within the eastern portion of the "Emerald Necklace," the string of Metroparks that drape around Cleveland, from "shoulder" to "shoulder." In the Metroparks, there's a choice of riding most of the way on either paved multi-purpose trail or on park roads. The return trip is on streets and roads that are mostly through suburbia, though in places the surroundings are more rural, and the route avoids the community centers, giving it an open, wide-ranging feel.

On a perfect weather day in July, Murray, Tom, my brother Scott, and I, assemble in the parking lot of the Sagamore Square shopping center, in the township of Sagamore Hills. This is the first time Scott has been available to join us on these Cleveland rides, but he's been my frequent cycling companion, riding part way across America with me on the journey recounted in my book *Roll Around Heaven All Day* and also a portion of my ride on US62, the subject of *Playing in Traffic*. Scott's riding a Trek 1500, while Murray is riding his Bianchi Brava, a road bike painted the classic Bianchi Celeste—a unique shade of turquoise with matching handlebar tape and water bottles. Tom is riding a Rivendell Blériot, an all-purpose bike designed around 650b wheels. Most road bikes today have 700c wheels, which is what Murray, Scott and I are running (and is close to the 27-inch wheel size of the old "10-speeds"). Mountain bikes usually have 26-inch wheels. The 650b, which was once a standard size on French-made bicycles, is smaller than the 700c but larger than the 26. I'm riding my trusty Sequoia Elite.

The Sagamore Square shopping center sits on busy W. Aurora Road/SR82, but we leave that highway after traveling just a tenth of mile eastward on it. We turn north off it onto a series of quiet neighborhood streets, with Murray directing us through the turns. Those streets lead us to Valley View Road, where we turn left and then right onto Dunham Road, continuing north.

Sagamore Hills is in northern Summit County. It was once part of Northfield, an original Western Reserve township surveyed in 1797. The area that became Sagamore Hills broke off from Northfield in 1932 and became its own township. It gained village status in 1943, but evidently decided that the earlier arrangement was better because it surrendered its village charter in 1947 and became a township again.

Two other communities we visit on this ride, Northfield Center and Macedonia, along with Northfield Village, which we do not visit, were also carved out of the original Northfield Township. Historians now refer to it as Olde Northfield to distinguish it from its descendants named Northfield.

Shortly after we turn onto Dunham Road, we cross Sagamore Road and enter Cuyahoga County and the village of Walton Hills. Like the communities formed from Olde Northfield, Walton Hills, Bedford, Bedford Heights and Oakwood are all children of old Bedford Township. Bedford broke from the township in 1837, becoming its own town. The other three split from the township in 1951, at which point the original township ceased to exist. We will pass through all four of those communities on this journey.

Dunham takes us to the entrance to Bedford Reservation, one of the Cleveland Metroparks. This is the point where, if we wished, we could start riding on the paved trail, which is just to the right of the roadway. Murray tells us that there won't be a lot of traffic on the park roads, so we stay on the roadway.

We hang a right onto Egbert Road and start climbing. We climb a bit more after we turn left onto Overlook Lane, but this soon levels out. Overlook tees into Gorge Parkway, the main road through Bedford Reservation. Shortly after we turn eastward, we come to a scenic overlook where we dismount for a sweeping view of the valley, with Tinkers Creek at the bottom. The creek is flowing westward to a junction with the Cuyahoga River, which empties into Lake Erie. As we proceed, the park roads follow the course of the creek upstream, though we can seldom actually see it for the forests around us. We continue on Gorge Parkway as it humps, dips and snakes through the deeply wooded park. Eventually, Gorge Parkway ends back on Egbert Road. We turn left onto Egbert, and enter Bedford, which is now a city, having achieved that status in 1930.

We proceed across Union Street and onto Hawthorn Parkway, which runs east-west through more of Bedford Reservation. In this portion of the park, we move successively from Bedford into Bedford Heights and then into Oakwood, and the parkland is uninterrupted by jurisdictional boundaries.

Hawthorn Parkway and the Bedford Reservation end on Richmond Road, where we turn north, crossing a bridge over Tinkers Creek. Our continuing journey now takes us away from the path of the creek, but later we will cross it again much farther upstream at the southeastern corner of the route. (On the Boston-to-Bedford Bikeabout ride, you'll see the western end of the creek, at its confluence with the Cuyahoga River.)

As we pedal north on Richmond Road, territory belonging to the community of Glenwillow is on our right. It was an unsettled rural area until 1892 when the land was purchased by the Austin Powder Company, a maker of explosives for mining and construction use, and later for wartime purposes. On the Glenwillow land, the company built a village to house its employees, and it eventually attracted other industries.

After three-tenths of a mile on Richmond Road, we turn right into the entrance to South Chagrin Reservation, another of the Cleveland Metroparks. As we do so, we are also entering land belonging to the city of Solon, which occupies twenty-two square miles in the southeast corner of Cuyahoga Valley. European settlers arrived in the area in 1820, and the township was named for Lorenzo Solon Bull, son of Isaac Bull, one of those settlers. Solon became a village in 1917 and a city in 1961. Although Solon has a large roster of industrial, commercial, retail and professional businesses, the community still has a sizable section of undeveloped land, some of it surrounding the metropark we're cycling through.

The reservation road is the resumption of Hawthorn Boulevard, and we follow it as it swings north. At the point where we go under the 422 superhighway, Hawthorn Boulevard turns east and so do we, eventually crossing SR91/SOM Center Road, so named, says Murray, because it passes through the original Solon, Orange, and Mayfield townships. Tom tells us that from the point where we entered the South Chagrin Reservation up to SOM Center Road and for another mile or so beyond, the metropark is little more than a sliver of green surrounding the road.

After crossing SOM Center Road, Hawthorn Boulevard begins a downhill run, and eventually enters a larger block of parkland, which is within the boundaries of Bentleyville. Being only 2.75 square miles, the village of Bentleyville is small compared to Solon, but 540 of its acres are devoted to the South Chagrin Reservation. The community is named for Adamson Bentley, a Disciples of Christ minister who came the area in 1831 and built a sawmill, gristmill, and clothing store while conducting services in a log schoolhouse.

Coming to Sulphur Springs Drive, we turn left and cruise down through more of the heavily wooded park to Chagrin River Road, which marks the end of our run through the Metroparks. We jog left onto Chagrin River Road and then right onto Miles Road, which, after about a mile, puts us in Chagrin Falls. We fol-

Glenwillow

In 1892, the Austin Powder Company, a maker of construction explosives, purchased land for a new home for their Cleveland-based company. Austin Powder soon developed a company village on the land to house employees, naming it Glenwillow. Occupying just 2.2 square miles in southeastern Cuyahoga County, the community became tightly-knit town, noted for its absence of crime and debt, and was thought of as kind of utopia. At one time, it was the only community in Cuyahoga County without a city income tax. Eventually the area around the powder plant became too populated for explosives production to continue, and operations were moved to Athens, Ohio. The Austin Glenwillow plant closed in 1972. A Village Center Project, launched in 2004, rehabbed the remaining structures of the company town into shops, businesses, and restaurants.

low some city streets to Main Street and the commercial center of town, where we find the Fresh Start Diner on the east side of the street. This restaurant has a seating area on the sidewalk outside, but it's a beautiful day and those tables are already occupied. So after parking our bikes, we find a table inside.

The Fresh Start has a good selection of sandwiches, wraps and salads, as well as breakfast foods available all day, and that's what attracts us. Scott and Murray both order pancakes, Tom has an egg-and-veggie wrap, and I get an omelet called "Evy's Veggie," filled with red peppers, onions, mushrooms, spinach, tomatoes and provolone cheese. We find breakfast food even better after a few miles of cycling, and we head out with full stomachs.

We leave our bikes parked and follow Murray across the street and a half-block north to where the Chagrin River passes under Main Street and then cascades over a 22-foot drop, giving the town its name. The community has provided a set of stairs down to a viewing area, where we get a good look at this scenic natural waterfall. After we climb back up to the sidewalk, Murray directs us into a store at the top of the falls, called the Popcorn Shop Factory. It's an old-time store selling retro candy brands that we remember from our youth, ice cream, and, of course, several flavors of popcorn. Murray tells us the store is widely known, having operated in the community since the 1940s. The building it occupies dates from 1875, when it served as a retail showcase for The Pride of the Falls flour mill adjoining it.

Next, we cross back to the east side of the street. From this vantage point, we can see another smaller falls, but this one appears to be man-made.

The falls drew settlers to the location and provided waterpower for flour, woolen and paper mills. The community became an incorporated village in 1844. Today, the quaint town, which includes many well-kept homes dating from the mid-nineteenth century and numerous small shops, has some 4,000 residents.

Returning to our bikes, we begin the second half of the ride. We pedal city streets to the south edge of town, and then pump through Bentleyville on Solon Road to the junction with Liberty Road, which runs due south for seven miles, surrounded by suburban and eventually rural housing. We follow Liberty its entire length, wheeling first through Solon. We are pleased to find that in the northern end of Solon, Liberty Road has a paved bike lane, so naturally, we use it, but as we move farther south, the lane ends. The road, however, bears moderate traffic and is not a difficult passage for the bikes.

Changing Gears

Fresh Start Diner
16 North Main Street
(440) 893-9599
Sandwiches, wraps, and salads

Farther south in Solon, right after we cross Pettibone Road, we notice a paved multi-use path on the east side of the road, but as the traffic is light, we remain on the highway. It's just as well, we decide, because after a mile, when we come to the end of Solon and enter Summit County, we see that the paved path ends at the county line.

Continuing south, Liberty Road is now the boundary between the Twinsburg and Reminderville.

Twinsburg, on the west side of Liberty Road, got its start in 1817 when 16-year-old Ethan Alling arrived from Connecticut to survey four hundred acres his family had purchased. He stayed on, selling land parcels to attract other settlers, and eventually he became the postmaster, stagecoach operator and hotel proprietor of the town, which was called Millsville. The current name came after twins Moses and Aaron Wilcox offered six acres for

Twinsburg

First called Millsville, Twinsburg got its current name when twins Moses and Aaron Wilcox offered six acres for a public square and $20 toward launching it, in exchange for renaming the community Twinsburg. Reportedly, these twins were so identical that few people could tell them apart. It didn't help that they were business partners who held their property in common, were married to sisters, and had the same number of children. Later, they both contracted the same illness and died just hours apart. They are buried in the same grave in a Twinsburg cemetery.

Capitalizing on that history, the community has staged a festival every year since 1976 for pairs of twins and other multiples, called Twins Days. As the event, held on the first full weekend in August, draws some 3,000 sets of twins annually, it has become the largest gathering of twins in the world.

a public square and $20 toward launching the first school if the residents would change the community name to Twinsburg. The community became a city in 1957.

Reminderville, on the east side of Liberty, was originally part of Twinsburg Township, but wasn't settled until the Great Depression when three Reminders brothers moved in. Eventually, about fifty families joined them. Because there was no direct road connecting their area with the rest of the township, the residents were concerned about how long it would take for Twinsburg fire services to reach them. Thus, they formed their own volunteer fire department, and the station became the center of social activities for the isolated area. In 1955, the settlement seceded from the township, and as the three Reminders families were well respected, the community called itself Reminderville. In 1957, the connecting road was finally built.

Liberty ends on Cannon Road. We turn left and plunge downhill to Aurora-Twinsburg Road/SR82, where we turn left again, work our way through another turn, and come out onto Ravenna Road, heading southeast. When we come to the intersection with Old Mill Road, we are at the extreme southeast corner of the route. Just before arriving at the Old Mill junction, we cross a bridge on Ravenna Road, underneath which flows Tinkers Creek.

Turning right onto Old Mill, we head west. Old Mill ends on SOM Center Road, where we jog left and then right onto Twinsburg Road, continuing west. While on Old Mill, and for the first mile or so on Twinsburg Road, we are in the community of Twinsburg. We then pass briefly through Macedonia and then into Northfield Center.

Changing Gears

Macedonia, settled in 1824 as "The Corners," received its current name when theology students from a seminary in Hudson came to fill the pulpit at the church in The Corners that had no pastor. The seminarians characterized the preaching invitations with the Bible verse "Come over into Macedonia and help us." The name stuck.

Shortly after we pass under SR8, we turn right and, directed by Murray, work our way through a series of streets and roads that "stair step" us north and west through Sagamore Hills until we come to Holzhauer Road. We pedal this a short distance north, where, right before the intersection with SR82, we turn into Sagamore Square shopping center, completing this wide-ranging circuit.

Miles and Directions

0.0	Turn right onto W. Aurora Road/SR82
0.1	Turn left onto Sagamore Hills Boulevard
0.3	Turn left onto Lynnview Drive
0.5	Turn right onto Brinmore Road
0.7	Turn left onto Orchard Grove Avenue
0.7	Turn right onto Paul Pine Road, which becomes S. Gannett Road
1.7	Turn left onto Valley View Road
1.9	Turn right onto Dunham Road
3.5	Cross Alexander Road (trail begins here)
3.8	Turn right onto Egbert Road
4.1	Turn left onto Overlook Lane
5.0	Turn right onto Gorge Parkway
8.1	Turn left onto Egbert Road
8.5	Cross Union Street onto Hawthorn Parkway
10.7	Turn left onto Richmond Road
11.0	Turn right onto Hawthorn Parkway
16.4	Turn left onto Sulphur Springs Drive
17.1	Turn left onto Chagrin River Road
17.2	Turn right onto Miles Road
18.4	Turn left onto Solon Road
18.4	Turn right onto Maple Street
18.8	Turn left onto Franklin Street
18.9	Turn right onto Washington Street
18.9	Turn left onto N. Main Street
19.0	Fresh Start Diner on right
19.0	Walk bike across Main Street and town triangle to Franklin Street. Remount and turn left on Franklin Street
19.3	Turn right onto Maple Street
19.5	Turn left onto Solon Road (stay on Solon)
21.1	Turn left onto Liberty Road
28.1	Turn left onto Cannon Road
28.7	Turn left onto Aurora-Twinsburg Road/SR82

29.0   Turn right onto Herrick Road

29.4   Turn left onto Ravenna Road

30.4   Turn right onto Old Mill Road

32.1   Turn left onto Darrow Road/SR91

32.2   Turn right onto Twinsburg Road

36.0   Turn right onto Anchor Lane

36.4   Turn left onto Scupper Lane

36.5   Turn left onto Foghorn Lane

36.6   Turn right onto Lighthouse Lane (Marked Highland Lane on some maps)

36.7   Turn right onto Olde Route 8

37.8   Turn left onto Marwick Drive

38.4   Turn right onto Brandywine Road

38.5   Turn left onto Meadowview Drive

39.0   Turn right onto Boyden Road

39.3   Turn left onto Forsyth Boulevard

39.4   Turn right onto Carlin Drive

40.0   Turn right onto Holzhauer Road

40.3   Turn right into parking lot of Sagamore Square shopping center

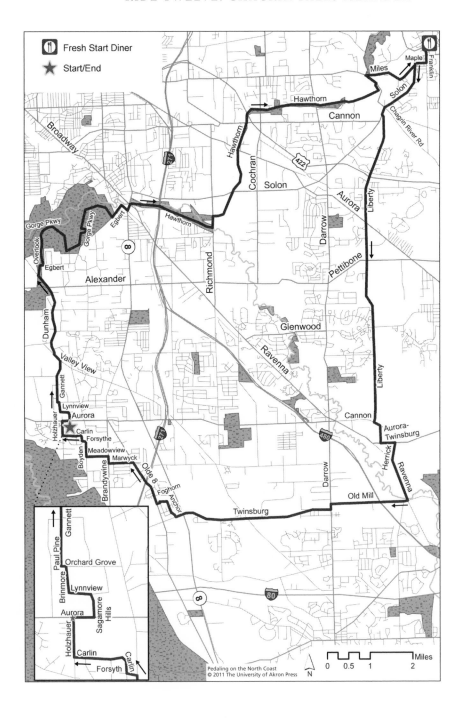

Fresh Start Diner

Start/End

Pedaling on the North Coast
© 2011 The University of Akron Press

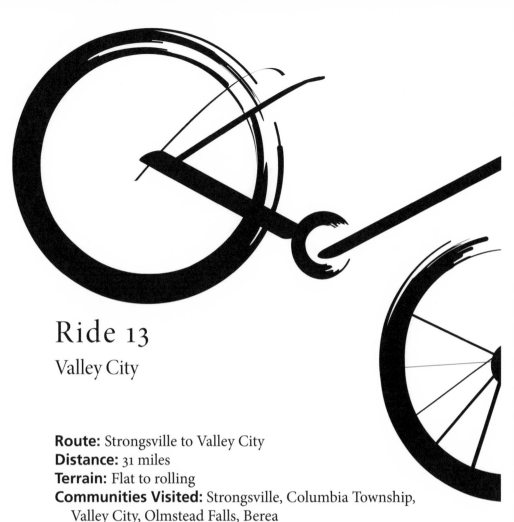

Ride 13
Valley City

Route: Strongsville to Valley City
Distance: 31 miles
Terrain: Flat to rolling
Communities Visited: Strongsville, Columbia Township, Valley City, Olmstead Falls, Berea
Starting/Ending Point: Bonnie Park Picnic Area in Mill Stream Run Reservation, on Valley Parkway at intersection with Albion Road (just east of Pearl Road intersection)
Points of Interest: Mill Stream Run Reservation, covered bridge, Valley City, Jilbert's Winery
How to Get There: Take I-71 to exit 234 (Pearl Road/SR42). Proceed south on Pearl Road to Valley Parkway. Turn left onto Valley Parkway. Turn right into Bonnie Park Picnic Area.

ere's a ride that ranges through three counties, parkland, suburban streets, rural roads, small cities and township centers, all in the scope of just over thirty miles, and includes Valley City, the "Frog Jumping Capital of Ohio."

On a pleasant day in late July, Murray, Dave, and I meet in Bonnie Park Picnic Area in Mill Stream Run Reservation and set out to ride.

Bonnie Park Picnic Area is set well back from Valley Parkway, the backbone road through the western Metroparks, so we pedal the picnic area road to the parkway, where we turn left, heading northwest. We cross busy Pearl Road/US42 at the traffic light and continue on the parkway. After about a mile, we come to Whitney Road, crossing the valley. We turn left on Whitney, through a covered bridge, and over the east branch of the Rocky River. We stay on Whitney as it makes a left-hand turn and becomes Eastland Road. A half-mile farther on, we turn right onto Fair Road, exiting Mill Stream Run Reservation and entering a suburban area of the city of Strongsville.

Strongsville is named for John Stoughton Strong, an early pioneer and land agent from Vermont who arrived in the area in 1816. It became a village in 1927 and a city in 1960 (the Big Creek and the Southwest Suburbs ride further explores Strongsville).

We proceed on Fair Road until it ends on Priem Road, where we turn left. Priem tees into Albion Road, where we turn right, moving into an area that feels more rural. At the point where we cross Marks Road, we leave Cuyahoga County and enter Lorain County and Albion Road becomes Snell Road.

Changing Gears

Columbia Township was the first European settlement west of the Cuyahoga River. Like many townships in the Western Reserve owned by the Connecticut Land Company, it was laid out in a block of five square miles. Land within the township was sold on a lottery system, which led to the township residents sometimes being called "gamblers."

Jurisdictionally, we are now in Columbia Township, which was the first European settlement west of the Cuyahoga River. The township was named by one of the first settlers, Sally Bronson, who called it Columbia after her Connecticut hometown.

The next turn we are looking for is Boone Road, which heads south off Snell Road, but when we come to what we believe to be the road, we find a signpost with the road-name sign missing. Murray, however, has ridden this route before, and he recognizes the turn from the large golf course—Emerald Woods—on the southeast corner of the intersection. We make the turn and are clearly in a rural area on a low-traffic road.

Boone brings us to Royalton Road/SR82. Boone continues south, but we must jog right on Royalton to reach it. Royalton is busy and there's no traffic light, so it takes us a couple moments of waiting for an opening to get across. When it comes, we don't dawdle. Once back on Boone, however, we are on a low-traffic course again.

It happens that both Dave and I had attended the Great Ohio Bicycle Adventure (GOBA) the previous month, he with his teenage daughter and me with my cycling buddy Wayne, and as we proceed, we compare our experiences. GOBA is an annual bicycle event that attracts some 2,500 riders for a week of 50-mile days that form a loop in a different part of the state each year. Wayne always likes to get on the road early, to beat the heat and arrive at the next location early enough to get a shady campsite. So each morning, he rousts me and another friend of his who rides with us at 5 AM and pushes us to get started. Dave's daughter, on the other hand, likes a bit more leisurely start, so while we all ride the same distance, his group arrives later in the day. Dave and I decide there are advantages to both arrangements, but we agree that GOBA was great fun, and we look forward to riding it again next year. Murray's not a big-event kind of guy, so he lets Dave and I blather on without interruption.

Boone ends at a right turn onto another back road, named Boston. Just before this turn, we leave Lorain County and roll into Liverpool Township in Medina County. Settlement of Liverpool began in 1810, but it didn't become a township until 1816. The small retail and commercial area at the center of the town-

The Great Ohio Bicycle Adventure

GOBA, an annual one-week bicycle loop tour through Ohio, has been held each June since 1989. Drawing 2,500 to 3,000 cyclists, it's a great vacation and excellent way to see Ohio close up. The daily rides average fifty miles, with optional extensions some days, through scenic and low-traffic areas. Participants camp each night in a park, school campus, county fairground or similar venue in the communities along the way and collectively spend a half million dollars in those towns.

ship was and still is sometimes called Liverpool, but in 1910, its Post Office name was changed to Valley City to distinguish it from the Ohio town of East Liverpool.

To reach Valley City (which, despite the name, remains a township) we pedal west on Boston Road, then southwest on Columbia Road, then east on Grafton Road, on which we cross the west branch of the Rocky River. We then turn south on W. River Road, and follow this into Valley City, where a couple of quick turns on local streets brings us out on Center Road/SR303, the main street of the hamlet.

While on Columbia Road, we have an unexpected adventure. With little advance warning, we come upon a location where a large culvert is being replaced. The old one is gone and the new one is not yet installed, leaving a deep trench perhaps fifty feet wide bisecting the road. There are no workers around, and the road is closed, with barricades erected and earth-moving equipment parked to prevent vehicles from getting any farther. This slows us down, but not nearly as much as if we were in cars; cyclists can often get through where cars cannot. We dismount and wheel our bikes around the barricades and heavy equipment and find that we can slither down the trench, step across the water in the bottom and clamber up the other side. We emerge with mud in our cleats, but glad we didn't have to detour.

Valley City is quaint, but when we get there we see three places where lunch can be had—Riverstone Tavern, Samosky's Homestyle Pizzeria and Eileen's Café. Murray suggests Eileen's. It's a homey place, and we get a table by the window. Although Eileen's has a lunch menu, they also serve breakfast all day. Murray has blueberry pancakes, Dave has fried eggs with home fries, and I have chocolate chip pancakes—a perfect "brunch" after riding and climbing our way to Valley City.

As previously mentioned, Valley City touts itself as the Frog Jumping Capital of Ohio. They host an annual festival for a day each summer when contestants of all ages—"jockeys" in the festival lingo—bring frogs (or even rent them on-site) for a contest to see which ones jump the farthest. A recent festival counted nearly seven hundred jockeys coming from across the country and as far away as Japan and Egypt, and even more spectators. The frogs are placed one at a time in the center of ring and "encouraged" by their jockeys to jump. Each frog gets three jumps, with the distance measured from the center of the ring to the frog's touchdown at the end of the third jump. The record, set in 1988, is nineteen feet, one inch. No one broke the record this year, but the winning jockeys received trophies.

Changing Gears

Eileen's Cafe
6699 Center Road
(330) 483-3598
Breakfast (all day),
lunch

While sipping his coffee, Murray tells us about the Jilbert Winery, located just a short distance south of the center on Columbia Road, which specializes in the production of honey wine. It's one of the few wineries in the nation that produces this product, and has its own apiary and honey-extraction house. It also makes more traditional grape-based wines and is open on a varying schedule for tours and wining and dining.

Finished with lunch, we head back north on W. River Road, which we stay on for ten miles. As its name suggests, it follows a path on the west side of a river, the west branch of the Rocky River. As we move north, road gradually changes from rural to suburban to urban. Initially it's a pretty country road, winding beside the river (which can see only occasionally) and humping over hills and dales. When we cross Royalton Road/SR82, we are in Columbia Center, the "town" area of Columbia Township. As we proceed, we see more mixed land use, but still with a rural flavor. After we cross Sprague Road, however, the surroundings become increasingly suburban. Soon thereafter, we enter the city of Olmstead Falls, where we turn east on Bagley Road, and cross the river.

Olmstead Falls grew beside the falls of the west branch of the Rocky River, whose waters powered a sawmill and gristmill starting in the 1820s. The community, which became a village in 1857 and a city in 1961, was named for early settler Aaron Olmstead.

After crossing the river, we turn right onto Lewis Road and then follow a series of residential streets, on which we eventually move into a residential area of the city of Berea. The last of these streets brings us back down into Mill Stream Run Reservation, where we turn southeast on Valley Parkway and pedal back to Bonnie Park Picnic Area, completing our excellent adventure.

Miles and Directions

Ride begins at Bonnie Park in the Cleveland Metroparks Mill Stream Run Reservation, 1/8th mile east of Pearl Road just south of Valley Parkway.

0.0	Exit parking lot, turning left onto Valley Parkway
0.4	Cross Pearl Road/US42
1.0	Turn left onto Whitney Road and cross covered bridge
1.3	At left bend, Whitney Road becomes Eastland Road
1.8	Turn right onto Fair Road
2.7	Cross Prospect Road
3.4	Turn left onto Priem Road
4.7	Turn right onto Albion Road, which becomes Snell Road
6.2	Turn left onto Boone Road (sign missing. Golf course is on left before Boone)
7.5	Jog right onto Royalton Road/SR82 and then left on continuation of Boone Road. CAUTION
10.2	Turn right onto Boston Road
11.2	Turn left onto Columbia Road/SR252
12.2	Turn right onto Grafton Road
12.6	Turn left onto W. River Road
14.2	Turn left onto School Road
14.3	Turn right onto Maple Street
14.4	Turn left onto Center Road/SR303 (Eileen's Café on left)
14.4	Turn right onto Maple Street
14.5	Turn left onto School Road
14.6	Turn right onto W. River Road (becomes Columbia River Road)
16.0	Cross Grafton Road
20.2	Cross Royalton Road/SR82
23.1	Cross W. Sprague Road
24.6	Turn right on Bagley Road
24.9	Turn right on Lewis Road (becomes West Street)
27.0	Turn right onto Fair Street
27.7	Turn left onto Meadow Drive
28.0	Jog right onto Prospect Street and then left onto S. Quarry Lane. CAUTION

28.2	Turn right onto Valley Parkway
28.8	Merge right to continue on Valley Parkway at junction with Eastland Road
29.9	Cross Big Creek Parkway
30.3	Cross Pearl Road/SR42
30.7	Turn right into Bonnie Park parking area
28.7	Turn left onto Aurora-Twinsburg Road/SR82
29.0	Turn right onto Herrick Road
29.4	Turn left onto Ravenna Road
30.4	Turn right onto Old Mill Road
32.1	Turn left onto Darrow Road/SR91
32.2	Turn right onto Twinsburg Road
36.0	Turn right onto Anchor Lane
36.4	Turn left onto Scupper Lane
36.5	Turn left onto Foghorn Lane
36.6	Turn right onto Lighthouse Lane (Marked Highland Lane on some maps)
36.7	Turn right onto Olde Route 8
37.8	Turn left onto Marwick Drive
38.4	Turn right onto Brandywine Road
38.5	Turn left onto Meadowview Drive
39.0	Turn right onto Boyden Road
39.3	Turn left onto Forsyth Boulevard
39.4	Turn right onto Carlin Drive
40.0	Turn right onto Holzhauer Road
40.3	Turn right in parking lot of Sagamore Square shopping center

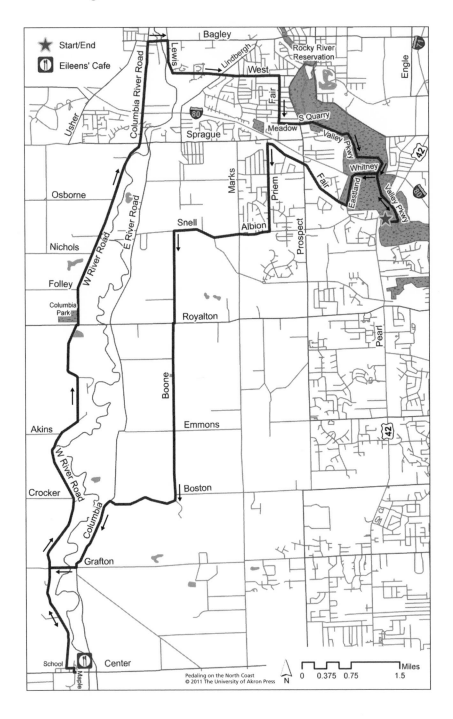

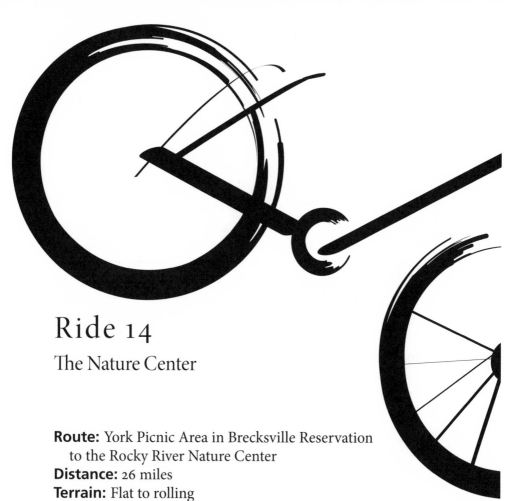

Ride 14
The Nature Center

Route: York Picnic Area in Brecksville Reservation
 to the Rocky River Nature Center
Distance: 26 miles
Terrain: Flat to rolling
Communities Visited: North Royalton, Strongsville,
 Middleburg Heights, Berea, Brook Park, Olmstead
 Township, North Olmstead
Starting/Ending Point: Ride begins at the York Road Picnic
 Area in the Cleveland Metroparks. The lot is located about
 an eighth of a mile west of York Road, on the north side of
 the Parkway
Points of Interest: Brecksville Reservation, Mill Stream Run
 Reservation, Rocky River Reservation, Berea Falls Scenic
 Overlook, Bonnie Park, Baldwin Lake, Berea Square, the
 Nature Center
How to Get There: Take I-71 to exit 231. Go east on Royalton
 Road/SR82. Turn right on York Road. At Valley Parkway,
 turn right (west) and proceed about an eighth of a mile.
 York Picnic Area will be on the right.

Here's an excellent ride for people who don't want to deal with traffic. It's entirely within the Cleveland Metropark system and can be ridden the whole way on a paved trail. While there is some rise and fall to the terrain, there are no big hills. At the same time, the ride is long enough to challenge recreational riders and give hard-core riders a workout. And because it is an out-and-back ride, those who decide after starting out that they've bitten off too much can simply turn around.

Nonetheless, if you do it all, you will start at the York Road Picnic Area in Brecksville Reservation, travel the length of Mill Stream Run Reservation and on into Rocky River Reservation to the Rocky River Nature Center.

Murray and I pedaled this route on a sunny but cool day in mid-April. Leaving our cars in York Picnic Area parking lot, we set out, heading west on the trail. York Picnic Area is the westernmost facility of Brecksville Reservation. In less than half a mile, we cross Edgerton Road and enter Mill Stream Run Reservation.

This is a good place to talk about boundaries. Not all of the reservations within the Cleveland Metroparks are physically connected, but several, including the three on this ride, are, or nearly so. A free booklet from the Metroparks, *Pathfinder: A Guide to Cleveland Metroparks*, shows where one reservation ends and the next begins. These boundaries are useful to know, but less important on the actual ride. The connected parks function as one big green space with a trail and road well suited to cycling.

The overlap is also true in the communities in which these three reservations sit. The tiny bit of Brecksville Reservation used by this ride is in the territory of North Royalton. Mill Stream Run Reservation sprawls over parts of North Royalton, Strongsville, Middleburg Heights and Berea. The portion of Rocky River Reservation used by this ride occupies bits of Berea, Olmstead Township, Brook Park and North Olmstead, but while in the parks, you have little sense of being in communities. There's one short gap between the north end of Mill Stream Run Reservation at Bagley Road and the south end of Rocky River Reservation, but the trail is continuous through it. If you choose to stop for coffee or food in Berea, you'll also see a small section of that city. But otherwise, you are in the parks all the way.

When Murray and I stop to wait our turn to cross Edgerton, I nearly fall over. We both use clip-in pedals and I have trouble getting my right foot unclipped. At the last second, I manage to get my feet to the ground. I dismount and extend the offending foot toward Murray. "Do you see anything wrong there?" I ask.

Murray studies my shoe and then responds, "Yes. One of the screws is missing from your cleat." Two screws are supposed to fasten the cleat to the sole. "But I think I have one with me," Murray adds. With that, he opens the "trunk" bike bag mounted on the rack over his rear tire, rummages around, and produces a small box filled with assorted screws and bolts. From it, he extracts exactly the right screw. We both have a small bundle of basic bike tools and the screw is easily replaced.

I have neither a trunk nor a rack on my Sequoia, just a small under-the-saddle bag, so I don't carry as much stuff as Murray does. But even at that, I am often surprised by what he's got in that trunk. On another ride, Murray realized soon after we'd started that he'd left his rearview mirror in the car. I thought we'd turn back for it, but Murray said, "No problem. I always carry an extra mirror." He opened his trunk, and sure enough…

My cleats firmly fastened, we cross the road and continue on the multi-use trail. We are not the only users of this path, but the trail is wide enough that we can pass both oncoming and same-direction traffic without difficulty.

Our continuing ride winds through the park, approximately following the route of the east branch of the Rocky River as it flows northwestward toward Lake Erie. We see the river only occasionally as the surrounding forest often blocks it from view. The passage is winding, and the trail occasionally moves from one side of Valley Parkway to the other, but it is not difficult to follow.

Eventually, within the boundaries of Berea, we come to section where there is a long, narrow lake on each side of the road.

The one on the east is Baldwin Lake and the one on the west is Wallace Lake. The lakes take their names from Berea's Baldwin Wallace College, which is a 1913 merger of two earlier schools in the community, one called Baldwin Institute and one called German Wallace College.

Shortly after passing the lakes, we see N. Quarry Lane teeing into Valley Parkway from our right. It's a short street that leads up to the Berea Commons area, where there's a choice of eateries. We'll visit the Commons on our return trip.

As we continue on the trail, we come to a short section where the passage squeezes between low sandstone walls, just wide enough for the parkway with the trail running beside it in sidewalk fashion, but the course soon widens out again and the trail veers away from the roadway and back into the woods beside the river.

Mill Stream Run Reservation ends at Bagley Road, which we cross at a traffic light. What had been Valley Parkway on the south side of Bagley becomes Barrett Road north of Bagley, and for the next quarter mile or so, we are in the previously mentioned gap between reservations. But the trail continues beside Barrett Road. A short distance after we pass under two railroad bridges, Valley Parkway resumes, branching off Barrett to the right, and the trail follows it. We are now in Rocky River Reservation.

Almost immediately, we come to Berea Falls Scenic Overlook on our right. We dismount and walk out on the viewing deck, which gives us a good look at the falls and the railroad bridges above it. As waterfalls go, Berea Falls is not very tall. It has two main drops and a few smaller ones that total perhaps twenty-five

Baldwin and Wallace Lakes

In the 1800s, Berea was known for the building blocks and grindstones excavated from the banks of the aptly named Rocky River. Its grindstones were considered some of the best in the world. That excavating gave birth to Baldwin and Wallace Lakes, as both are former quarries. Fishing is permitted in both, subject to special regulations. A children's fishing derby takes place on the third weekend in May each year at Wallace Lake. In season, park users can swim in Wallace Lake and rent paddleboats and kayaks to cruise on its waters.

feet, but the rugged rockiness of the gorge makes the sight quite impressive.

Back on the bikes, we proceed northward on the trail, occasionally crossing the east branch of the Rocky River on bridges. Just before we come to Cedar Point Road, we cross the stream one more time. Looking west from the bridge, we can see the east branch melding with the west branch, so that when we next cross the waterway, it is the main river, having gathered its tributaries for its final run to the lake. (The Valley City ride visits the west branch of the Rocky River.)

Changing Gears
Exhibits inside the Nature Center show how rocks form, what kinds of animals live in the wetlands, how Native Americans used the resources of the valley before Europeans arrived, the impact of glaciers in forming the terrain, among other things. For children, there is a structure that looks like the trunk of a massive tree, which kids (and grown-ups) can enter.

We come next to the Nature Center, on our left. We turn into and ride through the parking area and then pedal down the entrance path to the center, parking our bikes in the provided rack outside.

Inside, the center has interpretive displays, a library of books about the natural environment and a nature shop. We also see a structure that looks like the trunk of a massive tree; it's an

Native Americans in Ohio

When the first frontiersmen arrived in what was then Ohio Territory, they found several Native American tribes, including the Wyandot, Delaware, Shawnee, Ottawa, Chippewa, Potawatomi, Miami, Wea, Kickapoo, and Kaskaskia.

The pressure from settlers moving into this territory eventually led to warfare between the Native Americans and frontiersmen, coming to a head in 1795 at the Battle of Fallen Timbers. After the defeat, leaders of some of the tribes signed the Treaty of Greenville at Fort Greenville (now Greenville, Ohio), ending the war. In exchange for about $20,000 worth of goods, the Native Americans turned over to the U.S. large portions of the Ohio Territory, as well as territory in what is now Chicago and Detroit.

Although the treaty actually represented only a small number of Ohio's Native Americans, the government enforced it against all of the tribes. During the War of 1812, a number of the tribes sided with the British, and following the British defeat, their fate was sealed. After the war, the Native American population was gradually removed from Ohio, with the Wyandots, who made the greatest efforts to live like the settlers in lifestyle, religion, and dress, being the last forced out in the 1840s.

interactive exhibit that kids (and grown-ups) can explore while learning about park life. Outside, trails lead to Native American earthworks and a wetland habitat. The deck of the center overhangs the Rocky River and gives a good view of ninety-foot-high shale cliffs where fossils of ancient fish have been found.

Having had a good look, we hop on our bikes and set out to retrace our route on the trail. When we eventually come to N. Quarry Lane, we head up to Berea Commons, which is sometimes called Berea Square, though the small park in the center is actually a triangle. In any case, we have lunch at Sandwich Delights, a restaurant across from the square. (For more on Berea, see the Big Creek and the Southwest Suburbs ride.)

Finished with our meal, we get back on our bikes, roll back down N. Quarry Lane to Valley Parkway, and pedal through the parks back to our starting point, completing this enjoyable ride.

Berea Square

Café Ah-Roma
38 West Bridge Street
(440) 260-0286
A coffee shop with
sandwiches and bagels
*In the shopping center to
the west of the square*

Sandwich Delights
1 Berea Commons
(440) 234-3322
Subs and sides
On the square

Sweet Mango
54 Front Street
(440) 234-4816
Thai cuisine
On the square

Cornerstone Brewing
Company
58 Front Street
(440) 239-9820
Sandwiches, salads,
pizza, soups, entrees
On the square

Bucci's Restaurant
Berea Commons
(440) 826-4500
Italian, fine dining
On the square

Miles and Directions

Note: Mileages will vary slightly depending on whether you ride on the parkway or on the trail. The trail winds more than the parkway.

0.0   Exit York Road Picnic Area, turning right onto Valley Parkway

0.4   Cross Edgerton Road

2.2   Cross Royalton Road/SR82

5.4   Cross Pearl Road

6.7   Turn left at junction with Eastland Road to continue on Valley Parkway; do not go straight onto Eastland. (If you are riding the trail rather than the road, you will make this turn automatically.)

8.0   Cross N. Quarry Lane (Even if riding on road, trail use is recommended from here to Berea Falls Scenic Overlook) Or, to dine, turn onto N. Quarry Land. Then turn left onto S. Rocky River Drive to Bridge Street. Restaurants are on the square and to the left in the shopping center. Backtrack and turn right on Valley Parkway to continue route

8.9   Cross W. Bagley Road

9.4   Berea Falls Scenic Overlook on right

12.5   Cross Cedar Point Road

12.8   Turn left into Rocky River Nature Center

12.8   Retrace route back to starting point

25.6   Arrive at York Picnic Area

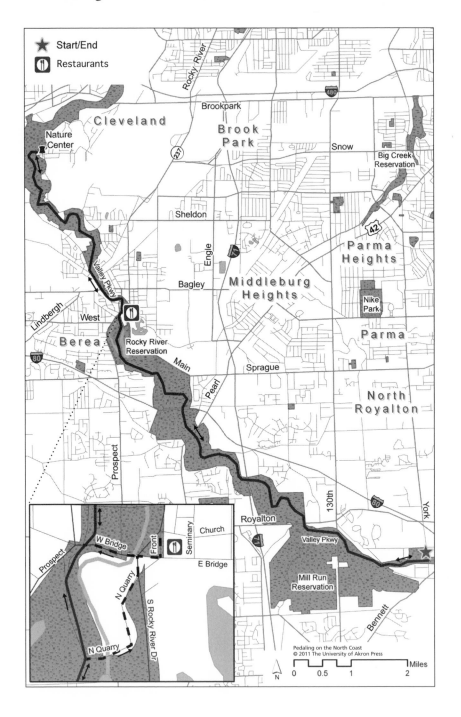

Ride 15
Aurora Farms

Route: Alexander Road Trailhead to Aurora
Distance: 39 miles
Terrain: Gradual climb outbound. Gradual descent
on return. A couple of climbs
Communities Visited: Walton Hills, Sagamore Hills,
Northfield Center, Macedonia, Twinsburg, Aurora,
Streetsboro, Hudson
Starting/Ending Point: Metro Parks Bike & Hike Trailhead
on Alexander Road, about 3.5 miles east of I-77 and 0.3
miles west of Dunham Road
Points of Interest: Sagamore Hills, Brandywine Falls, the
Brandywine Inn B & B, the Carriage Trade (buggy and
sleigh rides, catered lunches), Tinkers Creek State Park,
Tinkers Creek State Nature Preserve, Aurora Farms Factory
Outlets, Hudson
How to Get There: Take I-77 to Pleasant Valley Road
exit. Head east on Pleasant Valley Road, which becomes
Alexander Road. Trailhead is about 3.5 miles from I-77.

It's not every day that a bicycle ride uses a shopping center as a primary destination, but this isn't an ordinary shopping center. Aurora Farms is an outlet campus containing more than seventy stores, including shops for several major brands of designer clothing, shoes, jewelry, housewares, and gifts.

All the same, there's only so much room on a bicycle, and they aren't the ideal transportation for shopping sprees. Additionally, out of seventy shops, Aurora Farms doesn't have one bicycle shop. So why is this our destination? I asked Murray that very question.

"Because of the ride to get there," Murray said, "it's the oldest outlet mall in Ohio, and unlike most that are situated near Interstate ramps, this one is off the beaten path. As shopping centers go, it has an attractive setting. Also, the ride is nice and passes Tinkers Creek State Park and Nature Preserve. It also gives us a reason to ride from Cuyahoga County into northern Portage County, passing through Summit County on the way."

"A nice ride" was reason enough for me, and we think it will be enough for you as well. But if you need more reasons, here are some: The route uses a portion of the Bike & Hike Trail, which is a paved, multi-use path through attractive woodlands. It provides an opportunity to visit the gorgeous Brandywine Falls. It visits historic Hudson. Much of the ride is in semi-rural territory, meaning it gets you out of suburbia.

Murray, Tom, Dave and I meet at the Metro Parks Bike & Hike trailhead on Alexander Road on the second day of April. To our surprise, it turns out to be the warmest day of the year so far. It is 61 degrees at 10 A.M., when we start out, but shortly after noon, it's set to hit 80. We are cycling in shorts for the first time this year, and it feels wonderful.

We all notice Dave's Schwinn Range Searcher, a used hybrid bike he just got through Craigslist. He explains that he wanted a hybrid for the times he rides unpaved trails, although it also rolls well on paved roads like we are riding today. We look the bike over and hold our approval until after he tells us how much he paid for it. We approve, Dave got a deal.

From the trailhead, we aim south on the Bike & Hike Trail, which is one of the first "rails to trails" conversions in the nation.

More than thirty-three miles of the old rail route have been reworked to paved trail, but we are using only the northernmost five and a half miles of it today. (For more on the Bike & Hike Trail, see the Boston-to-Bedford Bikeabout ride.)

The first road we cross as we head south is named Sagamore, and at that point, we leave Cuyahoga County and enter Summit County. We continue on the trail until it emerges onto Brandywine Road. The trail resumes a bit farther south on Brandywine, but we will not need that section today. Brandywine takes us down a hill, and near the bottom is the entrance to Brandywine Falls. We can't see it from the road, but we take a quick trip of only a few hundred yards to a boardwalk that leads to a falls overlook. At seventy-five feet, Brandywine is one of the highest waterfalls in Ohio, and it is an impressive sight on this gorgeous day. We enjoy the waterfall for a few minutes and then return to the road.

We continue south, crossing over I-271 and then climbing a short hill. Murray directs us to turn east at the next intersection onto Twinsburg Road.

Dave has an errand to run and, as we come to "Olde Eight," he announces that he must turn back. We bid him and his Range

Aurora

Aurora was founded in 1799 after the land, part of the Connecticut Western Reserve, was drawn in a lottery by members of the Big Beaver Land Company, made up of citizens of Suffield, Connecticut. They sent a Revolutionary War veteran, Capt. Ebenezer Sheldon, to settle their land and act as their agent. After exploring the area, Sheldon brought his family from Connecticut and they became the first family in Aurora.

Other settlers followed, but it was cheese that gave the community its biggest boost. The traditional story is that in 1819, two young apple thieves skipped town to avoid arrest. They ended up in New Orleans, where they noticed English cheese selling for $1 a pound. After they came home to Aurora and squared themselves with the law, one of the pair, Harvey Baldwin, acquired a ton of cheese from local farmers and traveled down the Ohio River, selling the cheese at a profit. Learning of this, some residents of Aurora launched themselves into business, building factories to produce cheese in consistent sizes and grades that could command higher prices than the farm-produced varieties.

Searcher goodbye and wheel on. From here, Twinsburg Road heads downhill to where it passes under "New Eight" (SR8), a high-speed highway. We're glad we don't have to cross it at the traffic level.

Twinsburg Road continues through more semi-rural land and ends on SOM Center Road/Darrow Road/SR91. This is a busier street, but we simply jog north on it to the start of Old Mill Road, and carry on eastward. Tom mentions that he can remember when Old Mill was unpaved. We're thankful for the blacktop.

When we cross Ravenna Road, we leave Summit County and enter Portage County, and beyond that crossing, the land on both sides of Old Mill Road is predominately wooded and uninterrupted by houses. This is especially true after we cross a set of railroad tracks. From that point forward for about a mile, the land on both sides of the road is Tinkers Creek State Nature Preserve. Because much of it consists of peat, swamp and marshland, large parts of the preserve are inaccessible to foot traffic, but it's a great place for waterfowl, songbirds, beaver, and assorted other mammals and amphibians. There is a mile-and-a-half foot trail that includes a boardwalk through wetland areas. The entrance to the trail is from the south side of Old Mill Road just east of the railroad tracks.

Beyond the boundary of the preserve on Old Mill, Tinkers Creek State Park occupies the remaining ground on the south side of the road, to where Old Mill tees into Aurora-Hudson Road. The park has hiking trails, picnic areas and a fishing lake. We'll pass the entrance after lunch on Aurora-Hudson Road.

Tinkers Creek itself, which rises near the nature preserve, was named for Captain Joseph Tinker, the principal boatsman of

Chillicothe

Chillicothe was the first capital of Ohio, from 1803 to 1810, when Zanesville became the capital. The move to Zanesville was part of a state legislative compromise to get a bill passed. But in 1812, the legislature moved the capital back to Chillicothe, where it remained until 1816, when the legislature moved it to Columbus to situate it near Ohio's geographic center. There, it was to be accessible to most of the state citizens.

Moses Cleaveland's survey crew. In 1796, Cleaveland platted what became the city of Cleveland. Captain Tinker died in a boating accident while returning to New England in the fall of 1797. (The Boston-to-Bedford Bikeabout and Chagrin Falls Meander rides also visit Tinkers Creek.)

Changing Gears

Treichel's Grille
549 S Chillicothe Road
(330) 562-1773
Wraps, soup

Arriving at Aurora-Hudson Road, we turn northeast and follow it to its junction with Chillicothe Road/SR43. There we make a right onto SR43 and join the stream of cars waiting their turn to make a left into Aurora Farms. While we are in line, we see Tom suddenly swing left into the apartment complex just north of the outlet center. Murray and I stay in line and soon have our opportunity to head into the center. But when we get there, we find Tom waiting for us. He took an alternative route through the apartment's parking lot to an outdoor stairway in the back, where he walked his bike down into the Aurora Farms lot.

The stores of the "farm," occupying twenty colonial-style buildings, sprawl out over a large, landscaped campus surrounding a scenic pond complete with a gazebo and ducks. The stores include outlets from Adidas and Aeropostale right through the shoppers alphabet to Van Heusen and Wilsons Leather.

Murray directs us to a restaurant called Treichel's Grille, located in the middle block of the front row of buildings. We take a table on the porch, and are soon dining on chicken wraps and soup. Besides Treichel's, the only other dining option at Aurora Farms is a food court containing ice cream, sub, and pizza stands.

After eating and having a quick look around at the outlets, we mount our bikes and head south on Chillicothe Road/SR43 a short distance to Greenbriar Drive, where were turn west. Greenbriar is a residential street that delivers us to back to Aurora-Hudson Road. There, we turn south and soon come to the junction with Old Mill. Now, however, we continue past it, staying on Aurora-Hudson Road. We soon pass the entrance to Tinkers Creek State Park.

In the early days of the township, Aurora-Hudson Road was called Chillicothe Turnpike and was part of a much longer road, beginning at Lake Erie and running south to Aurora, where it turned southwest and ran all the way to the then capital of Ohio, Chillicothe.

Today, Aurora-Hudson Road's southwest flow is interrupted by the path of I-480, so as we roll near that crossing, Aurora-Hudson makes a right turn to cut over to a road that crosses I-480 on a bridge. Since Murray has previously scouted this route, we have no trouble identifying the turn, but otherwise it would be easy to miss because the blacktop we are on continues southwest without interruption, though it suddenly changes name and becomes Wellman Road. (The easiest way identify the turn is to watch for the David Round Company on the lower left corner of the intersection.)

The turn takes us to a junction with Frost Road, but to the right, is it called Aurora-Hudson Road. After wiggling around the Interstate, it again heads southwest. We notice that as we proceed and get nearer to Hudson, some of the signs say Hudson-Aurora Road. That may be because we have now crossed back into Summit County, but it's also likely that the naming priority changes depending on whether you live in Aurora or Hudson. In any case, once we enter the town of Hudson, the name changes to Aurora Street.

Hudson is a city with a village feel, especially since many of its nineteenth-century buildings, including both residences and the businesses on Main Street, have been preserved and are currently in use. The town, named for early settler David Hudson, was founded in 1802 and was the first European settlement in Summit County.

Western Reserve Academy

Western Reserve Academy traces it roots to the preparatory school launched with Western Reserve College in 1826. The college, modeled on Yale University and with several Yale graduates on its staff, operated in Hudson until 1882 when it moved to Cleveland. The preparatory school continued on Hudson campus until 1903, when financial instability forced its closure. It reopened in 1916 as the prep school and has operated as such ever since, drawing students from across the country and around the world.

A block before arriving at Main Street, we pass the campus of Western Reserve Academy, a well-regarded preparatory school that was founded in 1826 and now has students from twenty states and fifteen countries.

Hudson's historic Main Street includes several small businesses, including a highly regarded bookstore called The Learned Owl. There are also two restaurants—Hattie's Grill and Old Wedon Grille—that would be good alternatives if you don't want to eat at Aurora Farms. If you're in the mood for dessert, we recommend Main Street Cupcakes. (For more on Hudson, see the Western Reserve Ramble ride.)

We turn left off Main Street onto Owen Brown Street, named for the father of the abolitionist John Brown. (John lived with his family in Hudson from age five to age sixteen.) Next, we turn north on Morse Road, which takes us out of town. We then follow a series of semi-rural roads that put us on a northwest trajectory and eventually lead us back on Twinsburg Road. We follow this westward under busy SR8, but when we come to Olde Eight this time, we turn onto it, heading northwest.

Olde Eight moves through an area transitioning from rural land to suburbia, and there are a few businesses along the way. When we eventually turn left onto Valley View and then right onto Dunham, we continue through areas that are primarily residential. On Dunham, we cross Sagamore Road and re-enter Cuyahoga County, and shortly thereafter arrive at Alexander Road. We turn left, and within moments, are back at the trailhead for the Bike & Hike Trail.

John Brown

John Brown was born in Connecticut in 1800 but moved with his family to Hudson five years later, and stayed until he was sixteen. In Hudson, his father Owen opened a tannery. As an adult, John became so fiery an abolitionist that President Abraham Lincoln called him a "misguided fanatic." Brown's 1859 raid on Harpers Ferry, Virginia (now West Virginia), intended to spark a liberation movement, failed, and subsequently he was hanged for treason, but his actions were among those that eventually led to the Civil War.

Miles and Directions
Ride begins at the Metro Parks Bike & Hike Trailhead on Alexander Road, 3 miles east of I-77 and 0.3 miles west of Dunham Road

0.0	Enter Bike & Hike Trail heading south
3.1	Cross Aurora Road (SR82). CAUTION
4.5	Cross S. Boyden Road; jog slightly left to continue on trail
5.5	Turn right onto Brandywine Road
6.1	Cross entrance to Brandywine Falls on right
6.4	Turn left onto Twinsburg Road
7.5	Cross Olde Eight Road
9.5	Cross Valley View Road
11.5	Turn left onto SOM Center Road/Darrow Road/SR91
11.6	Turn right onto Old Mill Road
13.4	Cross Ravenna Road
15.8	Turn left onto Aurora-Hudson Road
17.4	Turn right onto Chillicothe Road South (SR43)
17.7	Turn left into Aurora Farms
17.8	Turn left onto Chillicothe Road South (SR43)
18.1	Turn right onto Greenbriar Drive
18.8	Turn left onto Aurora-Hudson Road
20.5	Cross entrance to Tinkers Creek State Park on right
21.3	Turn left to continue on Aurora-Hudson Road (watch for the David Round Company on the lower left corner)
21.8	Turn right onto Frost Road/Aurora-Hudson Road and cross over I-480
23.7	Cross Stow Road. Aurora-Hudson Road eventually becomes Aurora Street
25.8	Turn right onto Main Street/Darrow Road/SR91
25.9	Turn left onto Owen Brown Street
26.1	Turn right onto Morse Road
26.4	Turn left onto W. Prospect Street
27.8	Turn right onto Hines Hill Road
28.4	Turn left onto Valley View Road

30.1	Turn left onto Twinsburg Road
32.1	Turn right onto Olde Eight Road
34.7	Cross SR82
35.6	Turn left onto Valley View Road
37.1	Turn right onto Dunham Road
38.1	Cross Sagamore Road
38.7	Turn left onto Alexander Road
39.0	Turn left into Metro Parks Bike & Hike Trailhead

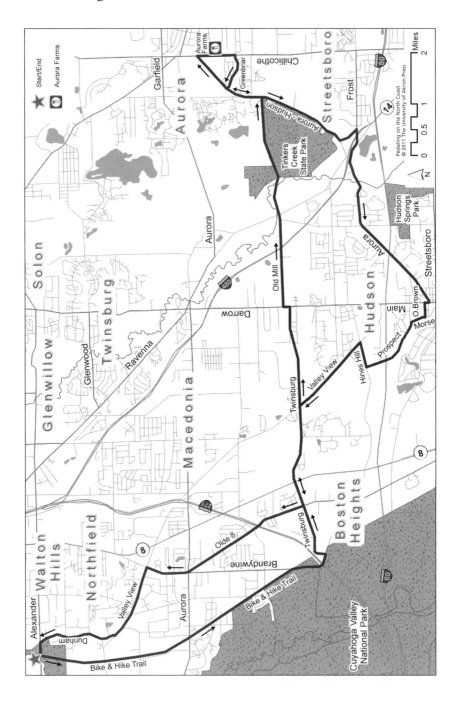

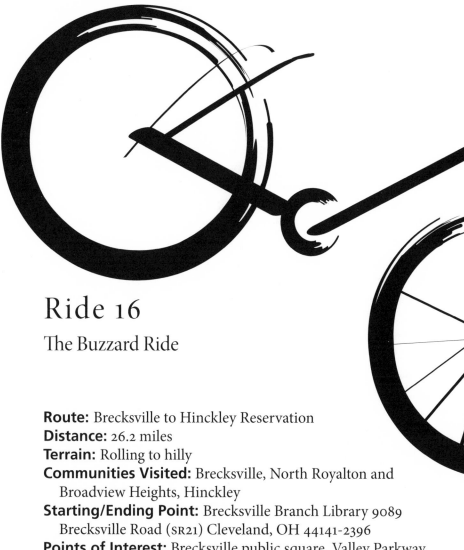

Ride 16
The Buzzard Ride

Route: Brecksville to Hinckley Reservation
Distance: 26.2 miles
Terrain: Rolling to hilly
Communities Visited: Brecksville, North Royalton and
  Broadview Heights, Hinckley
Starting/Ending Point: Brecksville Branch Library 9089
  Brecksville Road (SR21) Cleveland, OH 44141-2396
Points of Interest: Brecksville public square, Valley Parkway,
  Hinckley Lake and Reservation
How to Get There: State Routes 21 and 82 bisect Brecksville
  and there is easy access from I-77, I-480 and I-80 (the Ohio
  Turnpike).

W e've dubbed this one the Buzzard Ride because of the annual migratory return of turkey vultures— "buzzards"—to Hinckley Reservation every March 15. Depending on the season you pedal this route, you may or may not see these large birds, but at any time of year, you'll enjoy the forested Hinckley Reservation, which is the southernmost of the Cleveland Metroparks. The reservation includes a ninety-acre lake with a multi-use paved trail completely encircling it, as well as roadways suitable for cycling.

The ride loops from the city of Brecksville to Hinckley Reservation in the township of the same name. In between, you'll pass through park and suburban areas of two other small cities of the metropolitan area, North Royalton and Broadview Heights.

Brecksville sits at the crossroads of two major thoroughfares, SR21 (Brecksville Road) and SR82 (Royalton Road/Chippewa Road). Yet from the very first turn off the main street, this ride moves onto low-traffic roads that soon deliver you to rustic and rural areas. There is a good bit of climbing on this route, with one fairly steep and long hill on the return leg, so you'll get a good workout. According to Murray's altimeter, there's 1755 vertical feet of climbing on this ride, but don't panic. That's a total of all the climbing; this is a hilly route, but you won't be conquering the Rockies.

From April to mid-October, the snack bar in Hinckley Reservation is open, but during the rest of the year, the only places to dine or purchase snacks and beverages on this route are in and near Brecksville (as I found out the hard way).

First, a little about Brecksville. Founded in 1811, it was named for one of the principals holding the land, Colonel John Breck. The community incorporated as a village in 1921 and as a city in 1960, when its population surpassed five thousand. About three times that number call Brecksville home today.

The heart of Brecksville is the public square, with retail shopping around it and historic homes nearby. Should you need something for your bicycle before setting out, Velo Sport Bicycle Shop is located in the Brecksville Plaza on SR82, east of the square. Many of the neighborhoods sit near the Brecksville Reservation of the

Cleveland Metroparks and others adjacent to Cuyahoga Valley National Park. In fact, about a third of the community is parkland.

This ride starts at the Brecksville Branch Library, about a half-mile south of public square on the east side of Brecksville Road.

Shortly before noon, Murray and I wheel out of the library lot, heading north. It's a few days before the March 15 buzzard return, and after a particularly cold and snowy February, we are delighted to be on the road. Though spring is near, both of us are still riding our "winter" bikes. Those are not bikes made for cold weather, but older bikes we use during the salt-and-spray fest of winter roads in Ohio. Murray's winter bike is a KHS Urban Tourer, a hybrid bike with fenders and sturdy tires. Mine's a Trek 520, which is made for loaded touring (that is, with filled saddlebags, tent, sleeping bag, etc.). In fact, I have done a lot of loaded touring on it. But because it has a heavy-duty steel alloy frame, I also use it in the winter, saving my Sequoia for better weather days.

As we begin this ride, the sky is gray, but temperatures are warming and the forecast calls for blue skies later in the day. After a lot of gray-day winter rides, the potential for sunny ride even part of the way is especially welcome.

Brecksville Road, though a four-lane highway, is wide enough that we feel no threat from passing vehicles, especially since they are slowing as they approach public square. A block before the square, we turn left onto Arlington Street, which is residential and quiet. A couple of more turns and we are on Highland Drive and are starting to climb. The grade is steady but not severe, and we are easily able to ride up it side by side. After wending upward for a couple of miles, we turn right onto Valley Parkway, where the gradual incline continues for another mile before leveling out.

The parkway is the primary road through the Metroparks system (the "Emerald Necklace" around Cleveland). Farther west,

Valley Parkway goes through the heart of two Metroparks, but here, only the road and a few hundred feet of wooded green space on each side are parkland, belonging to the Brecksville Reservation. The trees are not yet in bloom, so we can see houses here and there beyond the branches, and farther on, the greens of Seneca Golf Course. Even without foliage, the strips of woodlands on each side of the road impart a parkland feel, and the 30 MPH speed limit keeps what little motorized traffic there is moving slowly, making the cycling pure pleasure.

Ready for a drink, I reach for my water bottle, only to discover that I have left it in my pickup. I mention my oversight to Murray, and say that I will need to purchase a bottled drink on the way. But Murray, who knows the route, tells me that there will not be any place to do so since the Hinckley boathouse has not yet opened for the season. He offers to share his bottle, and I accept, but I am concerned that there may not be enough for both of us for the whole ride. Even in cool weather, vigorous cycling works up quite a thirst.

Continuing, we cross Broadview Road, and the parkway slopes downward to where we pass under I-80, the Ohio Turnpike. Earlier, we had ridden a bridge over I-77. Though we are near these two major interstates, we intersect with them only momentarily, and the sound of heavy traffic quickly recedes.

Eventually we come to State Road (SR94) where we turn south. No longer on parkland, we are now rolling through a suburban area with houses spaced out along the highway. Off to the right, SR94 soon turns off, but we stay on State Road, which takes on a more rural feel. We pass a couple of barns, but don't see any farms. There are houses too, but this definitely isn't the suburbs.

We cross Center Road/SR303. Shortly before we get to the next crossroad, we top a rise (at about mile 11.7). By looking west between the houses, we can see the scenic valley below. Great scenery is the reward for climbing these hills.

The ride from there to our next turn is a roller-coaster-like route, which eventually brings us to Hinckley Reservation. Spinning past East Park Drive, we charge up one more slope to West

Park Drive, where we hang a right into the reservation. The field on our left immediately after the turn is "Buzzard Roost," the primary area for viewing returning birds. Since March 15 is only a few days away, preparations are underway: a temporary canopy has been set up adjacent to the road and portable toilets have been installed nearby.

To the right of the park drive is the paved multi-use trail, and there's nothing to prevent cyclists from using it. However, since hikers, dog walkers, runners, skaters and others also use it, cyclists have to repeatedly slow and wait for an opportunity to pass, so Murray and I elect to stay on the drive.

Pedaling deeper into the park, we come to a driveway on our right where a sign announces the boathouse and Johnson Picnic Area. We make the turn, roll down a short entry road, and within seconds, we are looking at the ninety-acre lake. In warmer weather, the lake is used by canoeists, kayakers, boaters, and anglers. When frozen, it hosts skating and ice fishing. The ice has only recently melted, so none of those options are open to us.

In season, the nearby boathouse rents rowboats, sells fishing tackle and bait as well as pastries, ice cream, snacks, and hot and cold drinks. Peering through the glass of the locked door, I see that the shop is also a Woolrich outlet.

Buzzards in Hinckley

It's not certain why the buzzards keep coming back to Hinckley, Ohio, or what drew them there in the first place. One legend says that the big birds were first attracted by the remnants of the Great Hinckley Hunt of 1818. That year, tired of the natural predators eating their livestock, Hinckley area settlers surrounded a large wooded area and advanced, firing their guns and forcing game into the center. Reportedly, three hundred deer, twenty-one bears and seventeen wolves were killed, plus numerous turkeys, foxes, and raccoons. Supposedly, the remains of the slaughtered animals froze and, preserved until the spring, attracted the buzzards.

There are other reports, however, that the buzzards were already roosting in the Hinckley area when the first Europeans arrived. Naturalists say the area is simply an ideal nesting spot, with ample water, fields, tall trees, and rocky ledges. No one knows how the birds manage to find their way back to Hinckley each spring on the same date.

Returning to the park drive, we continue toward the reservation's north end where the earthen dam impounds the east branch of Rocky River, making Hinckley Lake the largest inland body of water in the Cleveland Metroparks. The recent melting of heavy February snows has water racing over the spillway.

Coming finally to Bellus Road, we have the option of extending the ride about four miles by circling the lake. That is easily done by turning right onto Bellus, right onto East Park Drive, right onto State Road, and right onto West Park Drive again. The multi-use trail also encircles the lake.

Deciding to leave the extension for another day, however, we turn left on Bellus, passing a miniature golf course and driving range called Buzzard Cove. Like the boathouse, it is a seasonal business, so it is not yet open. A sign above the door announces "Refreshments," so in season the Cove is another place to eat.

Past Buzzard Cove, we turn north onto Hinckley Hills Road/ SR606, along which are spread attractive houses, spaced well apart. This whole region is the place to live if you want some acreage around your home.

Soon a momentary jog on Center Road delivers us to River Road/SR94 where we continue our northerly course. The gray of the morning sky is gone, the sun is shining, and Murray comments on the beauty of the day. When I agree, he adds, "And I can't think of any way I'd rather be spending it than bicycling." I agree with that, too.

Just beyond mile 17, we start up a long and steep hill that presents us with a mile and a half of climbing. Murray prefers to pedal up steadily in a low gear and he tells me to go ahead. I do and move up the hill, if not exactly bounding, at least with vigor.

Hinckley's Buzzard Sunday

Whatever the reason the buzzards return to Hinckley every March 15, the residents of the township make the most of it, holding a public festival the following Sunday, every year since 1957. Each Buzzard Sunday celebration includes a pancake breakfast, musical entertainment, storytelling, educational programs and, of course, bird watching. Visitors come from across the country to view the returning birds.

To my left beyond the blacktop, the hill drops away quickly—so quickly that the roofs of the houses on that side of the road are at about the same elevation as the roadway. Finally reaching the top, right where River Road tees into State Road, I pause to wait for Murray, who is only a couple of minutes behind me.

We turn onto State Road, retracing part of our outbound path, but rather than going all the way back to the parkway, for variety we turn right on Edgerton Road, which parallels the parkway to its south. Although Edgerton is residential and supports more traffic than the parkway, it is not a difficult passage. We follow Edgerton to Highland Drive to Valley Parkway to Brecksville Road and are soon back at the library lot—a bit thirsty, having drained Murray's water bottle on the way, but glad for the grand early spring ride.

Changing Gears

Hinckley Lake Boathouse
1 West Drive
(330) 278-3132
Snacks, hot and cold drinks

Buzzard Cove
1053 Bellus Road
(330) 278-2384
Refreshments

Miles and Directions

Start and end at Brecksville Branch Library, 9089 Brecksville Road, Cleveland, OH 44141-2396. Located a half-mile south of SR82 on the east side of Brecksville Road.

0.0	Turn right out of library parking lot onto Brecksville Road
0.3	Turn left onto Arlington Street
0.5	Turn right onto Elm Street
0.6	Turn left onto Old Highland Drive
0.7	Turn left onto Highland Drive
1.6	Cross Oakes Road
2.2	Turn right onto Valley Parkway
4.5	Cross Broadview Road
6.5	Turn left onto State Road
11.1	Cross Center Road/SR303
12.4	Pass East Park Drive on right
12.8	Turn right onto West Park Drive
13.6	Turn right to Johnson Picnic Area and Boat House
13.7	Return to West Park Drive
13.9	Turn right onto West Park Drive
14.7	Turn left on Bellus Road *Optional extension:* Circle lake by turning right onto Bellus, right onto East Park Drive, right onto State, and right onto West Park Drive again. The loop adds about 4 miles to the ride.
14.8	Turn right on Hinckley Hills Road/SR606
15.7	Turn right on Center Road/SR303
15.8	Turn left on River Road/SR94
18.7	Turn left on State Road/SR94
20.1	Turn right on Edgerton Road
22.2	Cross Broadview Road
23.7	Cross Barr Road
24.1	Turn left on Highland Drive
24.6	Turn right on Valley Parkway
25.4	Turn left on Brecksville Road
26.2	Turn right into library parking lot

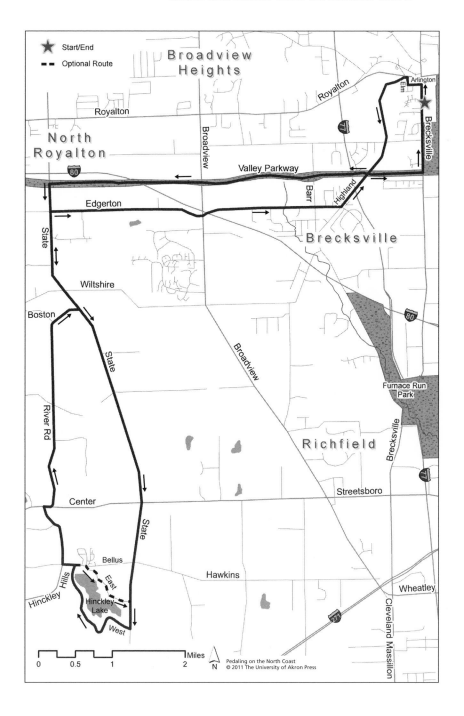

★ Start/End
- - Optional Route

Broadview
Heights

North
Royalton

Royalton

Royalton

Broadview

Brecksville

Valley Parkway

Barr

Highland

Edgerton

State

Brecksville

Wiltshire

Boston

State

River Rd

Broadview

Furnace Run
Park

Brecksville

Richfield

Center

Streetsboro

State

Bellus

Hawkins

Wheatley

Hinckley Hills

East

Hinckley
Lake

West

Cleveland Massilion

Miles

0   0.5   1   2   N

Pedaling on the North Coast
© 2011 The University of Akron Press

Ride 17
Western Reserve Ramble

Route: Brecksville Reservation to Hudson
Distance: 30 miles
Terrain: Rolling to hilly
Communities Visited: Brecksville, Peninsula, Hudson, Macedonia, Northfield Center, Sagamore Hills
Starting/Ending Point: Plateau Picnic Area. Within Brecksville Reservation, a short distance west of Riverview Road on the south side of Chippewa Creek Drive
Points of Interest: Virginia Kendall Park, Ski Area, Great Lakes Bakery
How to Get There: Take SR82 east from the center of Brecksville. After the passing the shopping center on the right, turn right onto Chippewa Creek Drive. Just beyond the junction with Valley Parkway coming in from the right, turn right into Plateau Picnic Area.

This ride starts in Brecksville Reservation of the Cleveland Metroparks system, travels through Cuyahoga Valley National Park, passes through the picturesque village of Peninsula, rolls out to historic Hudson and then returns via suburban and rural areas of Macedonia, Northfield Center and Sagamore Hills. There's plenty to see along the way, including the Cuyahoga River, Virginia Kendall Park, and the stunning Brandywine Falls. The varied terrain provides a good workout, meaning you won't feel guilty when you stop for pastries at the Great Lakes Bakery or for lunch at the Yours Truly restaurant in Hudson.

On a warm day in May, Murray, Tom, Dave and I gather at the Plateau Picnic Area to begin our loop to Hudson. The site gets its name because it's built on a hillside shelf beside Chippewa Creek Drive within Brecksville Reservation. We had to drive up a short, steep entry road to enter the area.

We are soon ready to head out. Murray is riding his Bianchi Brava. Dave is on a Trek 1100, a road bike to which he has added Suntour "Command Shifters," a short-lived innovation for changing gears. Mounted just inside the brake levers, they work something like today's integrated shifters and brake levers, but they weren't widely adopted, which is seems to be why Dave likes them. Tom, who has several bikes, is mounted today on a Rivendell Atlantis, a sturdy touring bike with 26-inch wheels. I'm on my Sequoia Elite.

We head out of the picnic area, turn right onto Chippewa Creek Drive and proceed through Brecksville Reservation. Although it is one of the Cleveland Metroparks, it is also part of Cuyahoga Valley National Park. The CVNP is comprised of both federally owned and privately owned land, as well as park units owned by Cleveland Metroparks and by Metro Parks, Serving Summit County, so there is a shared jurisdiction arrangement.

In less than a half mile, we turn right again, putting us southbound on Riverview Road. Riverview is the longest continuous north-south road through the CVNP, but one of four passageways through the valley. The others are the Cuyahoga River, the Ohio & Lake Erie Towpath Trail and the tracks of the Cuyahoga Valley Scenic Railroad. In an earlier time, the Ohio & Erie Canal would have been another passageway, but it's no longer intact. In places, it's a water-filled channel that looks much like it did in its heyday, but in other places it's an empty ditch and in still others, it is not visible at all. (For more about the CVNP, see the Towpath ride.)

The river, the trail and the rail line generally share the valley floor, but Riverview Road does so only in places. Other times, it humps over hills that intrude into the valley or runs on the hips of the hillsides. In fact, the first section of Riverview Road south of the Chippewa Creek junction has us climbing and plunging. The road is marked for park speeds and is signed to warn drivers to expect bicycles on it, so it's a good passage for us, and a scenic one at that.

We pedal along between woods and fields and pass a couple of small farms. Dave explains that those farms predate the park, but are now park owned. The occupants have agreed to operate the farms according to park guidelines and use only sustainable agricultural practices. Their efforts help the park meet one of its mandates, which is to preserve the rural heritage of the area in balance with natural resources.

Presently we come to an intersection where Vaughn Road comes in from our left. There are a number of wooden buildings at this junction, on both Vaughn and Riverview, all painted yel-

The Farms of the Cuyahoga Valley National Park

The existence of small family farms within the Cuyahoga Valley National Park is the result of the "Countryside Initiative" program, aimed at fulfilling one of the park's legislative mandates: to preserve and protect "the historic, scenic, natural, and recreational" resources of the Cuyahoga Valley, including the farming heritage. The initiative reactivates old farm sites within the park boundaries and preserves the farmhouses, barns, and outbuilding. Families are recruited to farm according to National Park Service guidelines and use only sustainable production methods.

As of 2011, there are eleven farms in the program, all operating in eco-friendly ways, while carrying on the farming heritage of the valley. At the same time, working with the local foods movement of Northeast Ohio, the farms showcase farming practices that minimize the use of herbicides and other chemicals. Farm produce is available at local Countryside Farmer's Markets, both inside the park and beyond. Volunteer workers who wish to learn sustainable agriculture practices are welcome.

low. Murray says that this Jaite Mill Historic District, the remains of the company town established in the early 1900s by the near-by Jaite Paper Mill. The mill operated until 1951, closing then because it couldn't compete with similar mills in the South. The settlement declined shortly thereafter. Other businesses used the factory for a while, but after a fire in the 1980s, it was dismantled. Its remains, including an old Fourdrinier paper machine, are visible from the Towpath Trail (see the Towpath ride).

Today, the buildings of Jaite look to be in good repair and house operations of the National Park Service. Tom tells about the yellow paint: When the park service took over the structures and removed several coats of paint, the bottom coat was yellow. So, in the interests of restoration, they applied the same color again.

As we continue, Riverview Road levels out on the valley floor, and we soon pass Boston Mills Ski Resort on our right. Across from it is a small station used by the Cuyahoga Valley Scenic Railroad. The winter snows are long gone from the ski runs, which are plainly visible on the hillside, but there are a couple of large tents on the lawn containing tables and chairs. Murray, Tom and Dave consult for moment and decide that this is for the Thomas the Tank Engine children's event, a feature of the CVSR. Thomas is a colorful replica of the fictional kid-friendly steam locomotive from R. W. and Christopher Awdry's *The Railway Series*. Once a year, the CVSR rolls the engine with its smiling face out to the Boston Mills Station at the head of its train to be the centerpiece of a day of children's activities.

Soon we come to the intersection with Boston Mills Road. Looking left, we can see the remaining buildings of the now-defunct Boston, a village established in 1806 that later became known for building canal boats. Today, the old Boston Store is a museum about canal boat construction. Adjacent to the store is an old gas station, preserved to look like it's ready to fill the tank on your 1940 Desoto. Across the street from it is a smaller store, still in business to serve park visitors. In the 1880s, a railroad station was built in the town, and the station was named "Boston Mills."

Continuing on Riverview, we pedal under two sets of high bridges, the first carrying I-271 over the valley and the second, the Ohio Turnpike. Under both bridges, we look to our left and see the other paths through the valley—the tracks, the river and the trail—side by side.

Eventually, we come to SR303, where we make a left turn and roll downhill into the village of Peninsula. The community took that name at its early nineteenth century founding because it was situated on an actual peninsula created by a horseshoe bend in the Cuyahoga River. The peninsula is no longer evident because nineteenth-century mill owners re-routed the river to channel waterpower. The opening of the canal in 1827 turned the quiet village into something resembling a seaport town, with hotels and honky-tonk bars. More peaceful today, the village caters to park visitors. Its short main street features antique shops, specialty stores, galleries, a bicycle shop named Century Cycles, and a couple of restaurants. One, Fisher's Café and Pub, is a local place. The other is a branch of an Ohio chain, the Winking Lizard Tavern. Both eateries offer a range of sandwiches, salads and specialty meals. Though we don't stop at either one today, I've eaten in both on other visits to the village; I had a bacon and spinach salad at the Winking Lizard and a grilled chicken salad at Fishers, both of which satisfied my hunger and my taste buds. In addition to indoor seating, both restaurants have outdoor patio service.

Almost without exception, the well-kept homes and other buildings give Peninsula a suspended-in-time look. After we spin through the small retail area of the village, we turn south on Locust Street, which becomes Akron Peninsula Road. This takes

Peninsula

The village of Peninsula was founded by Waterbury, Connecticut, native Hermon Bronson, who'd migrated to the area in 1824. The arrival of the Ohio & Erie Canal at the Peninsula location caused rapid growth of the settlement, but the village wasn't formally organized until 1837 when Bronson platted it and named it "Peninsula" because the Cuyahoga River wrapped around it on three sides. Its first industries included sandstone quarrying to supply stone for canal locks and canal boat building.

The village incorporated in 1859 with Hermon's son, Hiram Volney Bronson, as mayor.

us past a large golf course that extends as far as the intersection with Truxell Road, where we turn east. Still within the national park, Truxell ascends through forestlands for more than three miles, taking us out of the valley. Fortunately, it's a low-traffic road with a paved shoulder much of the way, and while the incline is continuous, it is not so steep as to be grueling. And the fact that we can talk with one another on the way up shows the effort does not leave us breathless.

While climbing, we pass the Boy Scouts' Camp Manatoc and entrances for various features of Virginia Kendall Park, another park unit of the CVNP. Because of the trees, we can't see much of either one from the road, but the Virginia Kendall Park is known for its exposed bedrock cliffs and ledges, which visitors are free to explore.

Shortly after crossing the national park boundary, we come to Appalachian Outfitters, a shop specializing in gear for backpackers, climbers and canoeists. It sits at the top of the climb, and we pull in so Tom can purchase a waterproofing spray for a bicycle jacket he owns. While we're in the lot, another cyclist rides in, and not surprisingly, he knows Murray, who is a fixture in the Cleveland-area cycling community. This rider is Jim Williams, and his bike catches our eyes. It's a Merlin, a high-end, lightweight cycle with a titanium frame. He tells us that he bought it a few years previously, shortly before his job situation changed and he decid-

---

Virginia Kendall Park

What is now the Virginia Kendall Park Unit of the Cuyahoga Valley National Park includes natural ravines, rock ledges, and deep forest, reminiscent of the Canadian north woods. In the early decades of the twentieth century, the area was owned by Cleveland industrialist Hayward Kendall, who used it as a rural retreat. Kendall died in 1927 and left 390 acres to the State of Ohio for a park, which was named in memory of his mother. Later acreage acquisitions increased the park size, and in 1933, a Civilian Conservation Corps camp was established in the park. The CCC crews built park roads, shelters, trails, and other fixtures. Virginia Kendall Park was managed by the Akron Metropolitan Park District until 1978, when it was transferred to the CVNP. There are three hiking trails within the park unit, which connect to several additional miles of trails in the CVNP.

ed to retire. "It's a good thing it happened in that order," he says. "I'd have not spent that much if I knew then that retirement was right around the corner."

As we continue talking, Murray invites Jim to join us, and he does, saying he can go as far as Hudson with us.

We five wheel out of the lot, pedal to and cross Akron-Cleveland Road, where Truxell becomes Barlow Road, and resume our eastbound trek. With the park now behind us, the scenery includes rural housing in the foreground. We stay on Barlow until just after we cross Darrow Road (SR91). At the next street to the left, pathfinder Murray directs us to turn, and then leads us through a series of residential streets that eventually bring back out on Darrow Road, but now in the city of Hudson, and having missed the Darrow Road traffic between Barlow Road and Hudson.

We turn right, and then follow Murray into a small strip of stores that includes Great Lakes Baking Company, one of his favorite food stops. We've all worked up a good appetite and welcome the opportunity to refill. Murray already knows what he wants; he orders ciabatta bread and a Monkey Muffin, which is a type of glazed cinnamon roll that is a specialty of the Great Lakes Bakery, and which Murray insists is "wonderful." Dave selects a cheese-filled turnover and an oatmeal cookie, Tom settles on a bran muffin, and I get a ham and cheese turnover and a cherry muffin with vanilla icing. Sitting at a table on the bakery's porch, we are a very satisfied bunch, eating pastries and drinking coffee.

Changing Gears

Great Lakes Baking Company
85 South Main Street
(330) 342-5878
Pastries, coffee

Yours Truly Restaurant
36 South Main Street
(330) 656-2900
Sandwiches, entrees

Hudson is a classic example of a Western Reserve town. Founded in 1802, it was named for one David Hudson, who moved his family to the area in 1800. The house he built in 1806 is the oldest structure still standing in Summit County. The community has a genteel, New England charm, and many of its buildings are on the National Register of Historic Places. It became a city in 1991. (For more on Hudson, see the Aurora Farms ride.)

As we remount, Jim says goodbye and heads for his home, which is in another direction. Murray takes the lead, and within seconds, we pass the aforementioned Yours Truly restaurant. He then guides of us through a series of city streets where we see older but well-kept houses. Soon we are rolling past Western Reserve Academy, seeing students on the fields and heading into the attractive campus buildings. One more turn takes us to Darrow Road once more, this time on the northern edge of the village. We ride north on Darrow in single file for a half-mile and then turn left onto Valley View Road.

Our continuing journey, including our passages on Valley View, Twinsburg and Brandywine Roads, is through rural housing areas of Macedonia and Northfield Center, though aside from signs on the highway, we have no sense of moving from one jurisdiction to the next. Macedonia, however, has an interesting story behind its name. The original crossroads settlement, started in 1824, was known as "The Corners." Not having a resident preacher in the hamlet, the settlers invited young theology students from Western Reserve College in Hudson (see the Aurora Farms ride) to come to "The Corner" to preach on Sundays at the village church. The seminarians began using the Bible verse "Come over into Macedonia and help us" (Acts 16:9) to characterize these preaching invitations, and eventually "The Corners" became Macedonia.

Twinsburg Road ends at Brandywine Road, bringing us back to the CVNP, at its eastern boundary. Just after turning north onto this road, we pass Brandywine Falls, a beautiful 75-foot natural waterfall in a rustic setting. The falls aren't visible from the road, but the parking lot is, and the falls are just steps away. You can see them from a convenient a viewing platform that you reach from a maintained walkway. It's well worth your time to stop and see this natural wonder.

Near the falls, with an entrance from Brandywine Road, is the Inn at Brandywine Falls, a bed-and-breakfast establishment. The inn was built in 1848 as the Greek revival home of a family that operated a mill near the falls. Completely renovated now, it's a pleasant place from which to explore the Cuyahoga Valley.

Eventually Murray directs us off Brandywine Road through a series of turns that step us westward, eventually bringing us out onto Holzhauer Road. There, we leave rural housing areas and enter suburbia. We are now in Sagamore Hills Township, and as we turn right onto Greenwood Parkway, we enter a housing development called Greenwood Village. Greenwood Parkway is aptly named; it's both a true parkway—a divided road with a landscaped median—and lined with trees and green space, giving the subdivision a pleasing park-like environment.

After a few blocks, we make a left onto Canyon View Drive, which takes us to W. Aurora Road (SR82). Heading west on this, we cross the Cuyahoga valley on a high bridge. It has a wide paved shoulder, so, if you wish, you can stop in the middle and look over the north side at the CVNP below. You'll see the river, the Towpath Trail and canal, the rail line and an area with dead trees that is the Blue Heron Rookery and the site of a nesting pair of eagles. Murray tells us that the pair gave birth to another eaglet this year—the third in a row.

If you cross the lanes to the south side of the bridge, in addition to the river, the trail, and the rails, you'll see the Station Road bridge, the Brecksville Station, and the Station Road trailhead.

A short distance farther on, Aurora Road brings us to Riverview Road where we turn left and roll downhill back into the park. We make a right turn onto Chippewa Creek Road and with a few more turns of the cranks, complete our ramble, arriving back at Plateau Picnic Area.

Great Lakes Baking Company

The Great Lakes Baking Company is a small artisan bakery located in the picturesque village of Hudson, Ohio. Since opening in the summer of 1998, the shop has produced a variety of freshly baked breakfast treats, pastries, desserts, rolls, and breads from scratch using traditional American and European recipes. Most recently, the bakery has expanded its offering to include croissants daily and pizza on Saturday nights.... The customer base is predominately retail, but the bakery is proud to acknowledge its bread, rolls, and pastries are served by several of the area's finest restaurants.

From the Great Lakes Baking Co. website

Miles and Directions

Ride starts at Plateau Picnic area in the Brecksville Reservation of the Metro Parks. The area is located on Chippewa Creek Drive, one mile south of SR82.

0.0	Exit Plateau Picnic Area, turning right onto Chippewa Creek Drive
0.4	Turn right onto Riverview Road
2.8	Jaite (Vaughn Road)
4.5	Boston Mills Ski Resort
4.7	Boston Village (Boston Mills Road)
6.3	Turn left onto SR303 Peninsula
6.6	Turn right onto S. Locust Street, which becomes Akron Peninsula Road
7.7	Turn left onto Truxell Road
11.0	Cross Akron-Cleveland Road. Truxell becomes Barlow Road
12.1	Cross Terex Road
13.7	Cross Darrow Road (SR91)
13.8	Turn left onto Argyle Drive
14.0	Turn right onto Beckwith Drive
14.1	Turn left onto Dongan Drive
14.4	Turn right onto Stoney Hill Drive
14.6	Turn left onto Sunset Drive
15.0	Turn right onto Bard Drive
15.5	Turn right onto Darrow Road (SR91)
15.6	Turn right onto Veterans Way and left then into small store strip to Great Lakes Bakery
15.6	Turn right onto Darrow Road (SR91)
15.7	Yours Truly Restaurant on left
15.8	Turn right onto Ravenna Road
16.1	Turn left onto S. Oviatt Street
16.3	Turn left onto Maple Drive, which becomes College Street
16.4	Cross E. Streetsboro Road (SR303)

16.7	Cross Aurora Street
	Western Reserve Academy
17.0	Turn left onto High Street
17.2	Turn right onto Darrow Road (SR91)
17.7	Turn left onto Valley View Road
20.4	Turn left onto Twinsburg Road
22.4	Cross Olde Eight Road
23.6	Turn right onto Brandywine Road
23.8	Brandywine Falls
23.9	Brandywine Inn B & B
24.9	Cross Highland Road
25.6	Turn left onto Meadowview Drive
26.1	Turn right onto S. Boyden Road
26.5	Turn left onto Forsythe Boulevard
26.6	Turn right onto Carlin Road
27.1	Turn left onto Holzhauer Road
27.3	Turn right onto Greenwood Parkway
27.9	Turn left onto Canyon View Drive
28.6	Turn left onto W. Aurora Road (SR82)
29.6	Turn left onto Riverview Road
29.9	Turn right onto Chippewa Creek Road
30.3	Turn left into Plateau Picnic Area

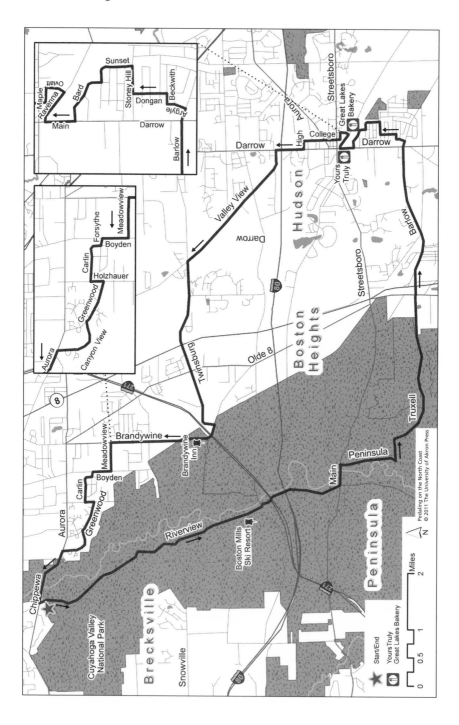

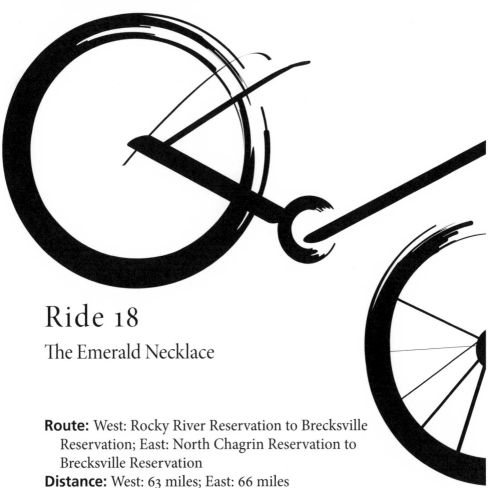

Ride 18
The Emerald Necklace

Route: West: Rocky River Reservation to Brecksville
Reservation; East: North Chagrin Reservation to
Brecksville Reservation
Distance: West: 63 miles; East: 66 miles
Terrain: Rolling
Communities Visited: West: Rocky River, Lakewood,
Fairview Park, Cleveland, North Olmsted, Brook
Park, Olmsted Township, Berea, Middleburg Heights,
Strongsville, North Royalton, Broadview Heights, and
Brecksville
East: Willoughby Hills, Mayfield Village, Gates Mills,
Hunting Valley, Moreland Hills, Bentleyville, Solon,
Oakwood, Bedford Heights, Bedford, Walton Hills, Valley
View, Independence, and Brecksville
Starting/Ending Point: Boston Store Visitor Center

Points of Interest: West: Scenic Park Picnic Area in Rocky River Reservation; East: Squire's Castle Picnic Area in Chagrin Reservation

How to Get There: West: From downtown, take the shoreway/us 20/us6 west. Turn left (south) onto W. Clifton Boulevard/sr237. Turn right (west) onto Detroit Avenue. Just before the Detroit Avenue bridge, turn left onto Valley Parkway and enter Rocky River Reservation. Scenic Park Picnic Area is at the bottom of the hill on the right.

East: Take i-90 east to exit 187. Go south on Bishop Road. Turn left (east) on Chardon Road/us 6. Turn right (south) on Chagrin River Road/sr174 and enter North Chagrin Reservation. Squire's Castle Picnic Area is on the right.

Greater Cleveland's Metroparks are a fabulous system of nature preserves—16 reservations in all, plus the Cleveland Zoo. Collectively, the reservations cover over 21,000 acres. They include picnic areas, shelter houses, nature education centers, fishing spots, boating waters, swimming holes, sled-riding hills, ice-skating ponds, stables, play structures, ball fields, golf courses, toboggan chutes, a dog park, a polo field and more. As you can see, "fabulous" is not an overstatement.

Changing Gears

Cleveland Metroparks is a separate political subdivision of the state of Ohio, governed by Cleveland Metroparks Board of Park Commissioners. The commissioners are three area residents appointed by the senior judge of the Probate Court of Cuyahoga County. They serve three-year terms without compensation.

The Metroparks also contain hundreds of miles of multi-use trails, cross-country ski areas and bridal paths, as well as miles and miles of bicycle-friendly roads. There are forty-seven communities within or adjacent to the Metroparks, so there's a park near almost everyone living in Cleveland, its 'burbs, and the bordering parts of surrounding counties.

The parks are reservations in the best sense of the word. Created in 1917, the park district aimed to make the natural valleys of the area "reserves" against commercial and residential development and provide recreational outdoor lands for the people of Greater Cleveland. Part of the official mission statement reads "Cleveland Metroparks will conserve significant natural resources and enhance people's lives by providing safe, high-quality outdoor education, recreation, and zoological opportunities." It doesn't take much time in the parks to realize that the park system has fulfilled and continues to fulfill this mission.

Because the Metroparks encircle the city of Cleveland on west, south and east (with Lake Erie being on the north), the whole park district is often referred to as the "Emerald Necklace." More particularly, however, six of the reservations, connected by a linear thread of parkways and public roads, form a "shoulder-to-shoulder" draping string of green around the city.

This ride runs through those six parks, but unless you want arrange for someone to pick you up at the end, you'll probably prefer to split the ride into two, with each half being a round trip of about sixty-three and sixty-six miles respectively. Thus, you can log a "metric century"—100 kilometers (62 miles)—on each. Of course, one good feature of an out-and-back ride is that you can make it shorter by either moving the start/end point or heading back before the designated turnaround point.

Other rides in this book have visited parts of all six of these parks, as well as several of the disconnected reservations. For that reason, we have not provided a narration of this ride. However, what follows are some ride notes for each reservation and the connector roads.

The Emerald Necklace West

This ride starts at the north end of Rocky River Reservation in the Scenic Park Picnic Area and extends through Rocky River Reservation and Mill Stream Run Reservation to Chippewa Picnic Area in Brecksville Reservation. Except for one section of Brecksville Reservation, there is the choice of riding either on the paved multi-use trail or on Valley Parkway. In that one section, there is no trail, so the ride is on the parkway there.

Rocky River Reservation

Rocky River Reservation sprawls over parts of Rocky River, Lakewood, Fairview Park, Cleveland, North Olmsted, Brook Park, Olmsted Township, and Berea, but the park rides as a continuous whole.

From the north end to where Cedar Point Road crosses Valley Parkway, the ride is frequently beside the Rocky River, which

Dining Along the Emerald Necklace West (Rocky River)

Beach Cliff Tavern
19245 Detroit Road
(440) 333-4686
Soups, sandwiches,
salads, wraps, pasta

Bearden's
19985 Lake Road
(440) 331-7850
Burgers, soups,
specialty sandwiches

Sweet Melissa
19337 Detroit Road
(440) 333-6357
Salads, wraps,
sandwiches

Danny Boy's
20251 Lake Road
(440) 333-9595
Pizza, pasta, ribs

runs northward toward Lake Erie and this is especially notice-
able when if you choose the trail. As this ride is in a gorge, in
places massive shale cliffs walls are visible.

Just below Cedar Point Road is the confluence of the east and
west branches of the Rocky River. From a wooden bridge on the
trail, just after crossing Cedar Point Road, you can look to the
west and see this meeting place. The west branch rises in southeast Lorain County and is outside the park (The Valley City ride
pedals beside the west branch). From the confluence southward
through the rest of Rocky River Reservation and on through
Mill Stream Run Reservation, the watercourse that the parkway
and trail parallel is the east branch of the Rocky River, which has
its source in North Royalton to the southeast. Below Cedar Point
Road, the river is visible less often from the trail and parkway,
due to the forestation.

There is some rise and fall to the land in this reservation, but
no significant climbing on the parkway. There are a couple of
spots where the trail climbs over the hip of hill, but these are not
lengthy.

Two especially interesting stops in Rocky River Reservation
are the Nature Center at about mile 9.4 and the Berea Falls Scenic Overlook at about mile 12.9 (both are described in the Nature
Center ride).

There is a small gap of less than a half-mile between the south
end of Rocky River Reservation and the north end of Mill Stream

Dining Along the Emerald Necklace West (Berea)

Café Ah-Roma
38 West Bridge Street
(440) 260-0286
A coffee shop with
sandwiches and bagels
*In the shopping center to
the west of the square*

Cornerstone Brewing
Company
58 Front Street
(440) 239-9820
Sandwiches, salads,
pizza, soups, entrees
On the square

Sandwich Delights
1 Berea Commons
(440) 234-3322
Subs and sides
On the square

Sweet Mango
54 Front Street
(440) 234-4816
Thai cuisine
On the square

Bucci's Restaurant
1 Berea Commons
(440) 826-4500
Italian, fine dining
On the square

Run Reservation. If you are using the road, you'll need to pedal on a city street named Barrett, which isn't quite as bike friendly as the parkway. But the trail is continuous through this section, so even if you are biking on the parkway, we recommend that you use the trail starting at the Berea Falls Scenic Overlook to at least Bagley Road, where you enter Mill Stream Run Reservation.

Mill Stream Run Reservation

Mill Stream Run Reservation stretches through parts of Berea, Middleburg Heights, Strongsville, and North Royalton. The east branch of the Rocky River is the backbone that runs through the reservation. Though the river is visible only occasionally from the trail and the parkway, those two paths mostly follow its course.

The city square area of Berea, accessed from the parkway via N. Quarry Lane, has several places for dining. (For more about Berea, see the Big Creek and Nature Center rides.)

The rocky nature of the riverbanks gave rise to a building-block and grindstone mining industry in Berea in the nineteenth and early twentieth centuries. A short way below N. Quarry Lane, the parkway passes between two lakes, Baldwin on the east and Wallace on the west. Both of these were originally quarries where grindstones, considered some of the finest in the world, were excavated. In the summer, Wallace Lake is open for swimming, boating, fishing and paddleboat rental. In the winter, it's used for ice skating, and ice-fishing. Fishing is permitted in Baldwin Lake.

Dining Along the Emerald Necklace West (Brecksville)

The Courtyard
7600 Chippewa Road
(440) 526-9292
Pizza, salads, pasta,
fish, burgers, ribs, steaks

Sakura's Restaurant
8409 Chippewa Road
(440) 526-3300
Japanese, sushi

Simon's Restaurant & Deli
7770 Chippewa Road
(440) 526-6880
Bistro and deli foods

Panera Bread
8447 Chippewa Road
(440) 717-1437
Salads, soups, sandwiches

This reservation is aligned northwest to southeast, with Berea at its northwest end. For the rest of the way through the park, it is heavily wooded, punctuated with picnic areas and broken only by the occasional crossroad. The ride on both parkway and the trail is relatively flat throughout this park.

At the southeast end of the reservation, the east branch of the Rocky River continues in that direction, but the trail and the parkway swing west. Where they cross Edgerton Road, Mill Stream Run Reservation ends and Brecksville Reservation starts.

Brecksville Reservation

Brecksville Reservation extends through North Royalton, Broadview Heights and Brecksville. From Edgerton Road on its west end, it runs due east to Brecksville Road/SR21 as a thin corridor of green, through which the parkway unrolls. The multiuse trail runs through part of that passage, but ends just before Ridge Road crosses the parkway. There are two picnic areas in the corridor, York Road Picnic Area near the west end of the park and Stuhr Woods Picnic Area, across the parkway from where the trail ends.

The main body of the reservation starts east of Brecksville Road and reaches to Riverview Road where the reservation links with Cuyahoga Valley National Park. The multi-use trail resumes at Brecksville Road and continues to Riverview Road. There are several picnic areas in the main section.

Though the corridor section of the reservation is narrow, there is enough woodland on both sides of the road to separate park users from the neighborhoods beyond.

In terms of cycling the Emerald Necklace West, this corridor section is the hilliest, with one significant climb between Bennett and Ridge Roads, and a few smaller ones between Ridge and Brecksville Roads. In terms of geography, the corridor travels over the hump between the east branch of the Rocky River valley and the Cuyahoga River valley. (The Buzzard Ride ride includes a portion of this corridor.)

Once across Brecksville Road, however, there's a glorious downhill run all the way to Chippewa Creek Drive. Turn left there, and then left again almost immediately into Chippewa Picnic Area, the turnaround point for the ride.

Before plunging down Valley Parkway from Brecksville Road, it's good to decide if you want to stop for lunch. If so, you may prefer to turn left onto Brecksville Road and ride the short distance to downtown Brecksville. There, at the center of town, you can turn right onto Chippewa Road/SR82, where there are restaurants in shopping centers on both sides of the road. After eating, you can reach the Chippewa Picnic Area turnaround point without backtracking. Just continue beyond the shopping center on Chippewa Road and turn right onto Chippewa Creek Drive. Continue on that for 1.2 miles. The picnic area will be on the right.

If you prefer to complete the ride before eating, you can then reach the restaurants by turning left out of Chippewa Picnic Area onto Chippewa Creek Drive and follow it to Chippewa Road/ SR82. Turn left onto Chippewa Road. Be aware that from Chippewa Picnic Area to the shopping center area is an uphill ride.

The Emerald Necklace East

This ride begins at the Squire's Castle Picnic Area in North Chagrin Reservation and travels southward through the Chagrin River valley to South Chagrin Reservation. From there, it steps west and south following Hawthorne Parkway and then Gorge Parkway through Bedford Reservation. After that reservation, it continues west and south through the Cuyahoga Valley National Park, and ends at Chippewa Picnic Area in Brecksville Reservation. There is a choice of road or multi-use trail for some of the passage, but where road is the only option, the course is still bicycle-friendly. The multi-use trail is available starting in South Chagrin Reservation at Sulphur Springs Road and continuing (except for a couple of on-road jogs) into Bedford Reservation to the junction with Overlook Lane.

North Chagrin Reservation

North Chagrin Reservation, set aside as a preserve in the 1920s, spreads across parts of Willoughby Hills, Mayfield Village and Gates Mills.

Squire's Castle, at the start point, is a stone building with turrets and battlements, looking indeed like a small medieval castle. It was built in the 1890s by industrialist F. B. Squire as the gatehouse for a country estate, but the estate itself was never constructed. The castle has no doors and is constantly open for visitors. Plaques inside tell the story of the estate. (The Chagrin Valley ride also visits Squire's Castle.)

The passage through the park is on Chagrin River Road. While there is some paved multi-use trail elsewhere in this reservation, there is none along Chagrin River Road. As its name suggests, this road roughly parallels the course of the Chagrin River. The river flows north toward Lake Erie. Heading south, the road is first on the west side of the river and then, below the Wilson Mills Road crossing, on the east side. There is a little climbing on this road, but nothing major. When you cross Mayfield Road, you leave the reservation.

Chagrin River Road

Once outside of North Chagrin Reservation, the journey continues on Chagrin River Road, which heads due south toward South Chagrin Reservation. In the 1940s, there was a move to make the road between the two reservations a parkway, but that required the consent of the villages along the way. In 1943, the citizens of Gates Mills defeated the proposal, so the road remains a public highway, though pastoral and rural in character, with

---

Dining Along the Emerald Necklace East (Chagrin Falls & Valley View)

Chagrin Falls

Fresh Start Diner
16 North Main Street
(440) 893-9599
Sandwiches, wraps, salads, fast foods available all day

Joey's Restaurant
44 North Main Street
(440) 247-6085
Italian food

Yours Truly Restaurant
30 North Main Street
(440) 247-3232
Sandwiches, salads, breakomelets, entrees

Valley View
Tinkers Creek Road Tavern
14000 Tinkers Creek Road
(216) 642-3900
Sandwiches, salads, entrees

Brecksville is also a good destination for food. See previous box.

relatively low traffic levels. The main drawback for cyclists is the requirement to ride single file, which is not a great hardship, but it does hamper conversation when riding with others.

As this road proceeds south, it passes through, successively, Gates Mills, Hunting Valley, and Moreland Hills, all of it horse country. This is especially apparent in the village center of Gates Mills, home to Chagrin Valley Hunt Club. Unless you detour into the village center, you won't see this, however, as Chagrin River Road bypasses most of it. But there are bridle paths, stables and horse workout yards elsewhere along the road.

Near the Gates Mills village center, Chagrin River Road crosses a bridge, moving back to the west bank of the river, where it stays for the rest of the time on this road.

South Chagrin Reservation begins where Chagrin River Road crosses Kinsman Road/SR87.

South Chagrin Reservation

South Chagrin Reservation is located in Moreland Hills, Bentleyville and Solon, but the route through it is entirely in parkland.

Shortly after entering the reservation, there is a polo field on the east side of Chagrin River Road. This is a good start point if you want a shorter ride. A round trip from the polo field to the turnaround point—Chippewa Picnic Area in Brecksville Reservation—is about forty-six miles.

After crossing Miles Road, the route continues south on Sulphur Springs Drive. There is a stout climb on Sulphur Springs Drive that continues after the turn westward onto Hawthorn Parkway, cresting near the SOM Center Road/SR91 crossing. Part way up the hill on Hawthorn Parkway, the reservation narrows down to a green sliver of parkland that continues west to about where US422 passes over the parkway. From there, the parkway and the "sliver" turn south and then finally west again to the junction with Richmond Road.

For more on North Chagrin and South Chagrin Reservations, and Chagrin River Road between them, see the Chagrin Valley ride.

Bedford Reservation

Brecksville Reservation covers parts of the communities of Oakwood, Bedford Heights and Bedford, Walton Hills and Valley View.

A short jog southward on Richmond Road connects the ride from the exit from South Chagrin Reservation to Bedford Reservation and the continuation of Hawthorne Parkway. Bedford Reservation has two sections. The portion from Richmond Road to Union Street is a slender east-west piece of land, and the road through it is Hawthorne Parkway. The larger portion of the park starts at Union Street and stretches westward. The road through most of this portion is Gorge Parkway, which runs on the bluff above Tinkers Creek.

There is a scenic overlook on the north side of Gorge Parkway at about mile twenty-four that provides a stunning view of the gorge and the creek.

After crossing Overlook Lane, Gorge Parkway plunges downhill to the bank of the Creek below. Gorge Parkway and Bedford Reservation end at Dunham Road.

For more information about the route from South Chagrin Reservation to Bedford Reservation, see the Chagrin Falls Meander ride.

Cuyahoga Valley National Park

The national park includes parts of several communities, but the section used by this ride is in Valley View, Independence, and Brecksville.

The ride route continues west on Tinkers Creek Road. While a bike-friendly course, Tinkers Creek Road is not parkway, and has houses on both sides. Tinkers Creek Road Tavern, an option for dining, is on the left at about mile 25.8.

From Tinkers Creek Road, the ride turns south on Canal Road, which is right beside the old Ohio & Erie Canal, with the Towpath Trail on the opposite bank. Eventually, an exit ramp from Canal Road leads up to where Alexander/Pleasant Valley Road crosses above Canal Road, the canal and Towpath, the river and the rail line used by the Cuyahoga Valley Scenic Railroad.

The ride turns west on Pleasant Valley Road to Brookside Road and the northern terminus of Riverview Road. It turns south on Riverview.

There are two hills to climb on Riverview before reaching Chippewa Road/SR82. After crossing Chippewa Road, Riverview runs steeply down a short hill and into Brecksville Reservation.

For more on the ride from Bedford Reservation through the Cuyahoga Valley National Park, see the Boston-to-Bedford Bike-about ride.

Brecksville Reservation

The junction with Chippewa Creek Drive is at the bottom of the Riverview Road hill. Chippewa Picnic Area, where the ride ends, is a half mile west on this road.

For lunch, continue west on Chippewa Creek Drive for 1.2 miles to Chippewa Road/SR82. Turn left. Restaurants are in the shopping centers on both sides of the road.

Build Your Own Ride

As already mentioned, out-and-back routes lend themselves to tailored rides and the Emerald Necklace is the perfect place for a create-your-own journey. With the many parking areas throughout the Metroparks, you have numerous options for where to start a ride, and when you turn around, you'll always know how far it is back to your vehicle. Cyclists seeking a truly long-distance ride can pedal the entire Emerald Necklace ride from end to end and back, logging 129 miles. But riders can also have fun on much shorter rides, and the Cleveland Metroparks system provides plenty of natural scenery and paved surfaces to make the six, sixty, or any chosen number of miles ridden in them a great pleasure.

Miles and Directions

Note: All mileages are clocked from the parkways and roads. If you ride the multi-use trail, the mileage may vary slightly, due to its winding route.

The Emerald Necklace West

Ride begins at the Scenic Park Picnic Area on Valley Parkway, just south of Detroit Road in Rocky River Reservation

0.0	Turn right out of Scenic Park Picnic Area, heading south on Valley Parkway (or on the parallel multi-purpose trail)
9.8	Cross Cedar Point Road
12.9	Berea Falls Scenic Overlook (Even if riding on road, trail use is recommended from here to N. Quarry Road)
13.4	Cross Bagley Road and enter Mill Stream Run Reservation
14.3	Cross N. Quarry Road (or, for dining, turn left on N. Quarry and follow it to shopping area in Berea)
15.4	Turn right at junction with Easton Road to continue on Valley Parkway
16.9	Cross Pearl Road/US 42
20.1	Cross Royalton Road/SR82
21.9	Cross Edgerton Road
24.3	Cross State Road/SR94
29.3	Cross Brecksville Road/SR21 and enter Brecksville Reservation OR, to dine, turn left and go to downtown Brecksville. Turn right onto Chippewa Road/SR82. Restaurants on right are Simon's and the Courtyard; on the left are Panera Bread and Sakura's. After eating, continue a short distance east beyond the shopping centers on Chippewa Road and turn right onto Chippewa Creek Drive. Continue for 1.2 miles to Chippewa Picnic Area, on the right
31.2	Turn left onto Chippewa Creek Drive
31.3	Turn left into Chippewa Picnic Area Retrace route to start point

Or, to continue the Necklace:

0.0	Exit Chippewa Picnic Area, turning right onto Chippewa Creek Drive

0.5	Turn left onto Riverview Road
0.7	Cross Chippewa Road/SR82
3.8	Turn right onto Brookside Road
3.9	Turn right onto Pleasant Valley Road
4.5	Turn right onto Canal Road entrance ramp to drop down to Canal Road
4.6	Turn right onto Canal Road
5.5	Turn right onto Tinkers Creek Road (Tinker's Creek Tavern is on this road, on the right side, just before Dunham Road junction)
7.2	Turn right onto Dunham Road
7.3	Turn left onto Gorge Parkway
8.4	Cross Overlook Lane
11.5	Turn left onto Egbert Road
11.9	Cross Union Street onto Bedford/Chagrin/Hawthorn Parkway
14.1	Turn left onto Richmond Road
14.4	Turn right onto Hawthorn Parkway
19.8	Turn left onto Sulphur Springs Drive
20.5	Turn left onto Chagrin River Road
20.6	Cross Miles Road and head north on Chagrin River Road (only single-file riding permitted on Chagrin River Road)
23.0	Cross Polo Field
28.0	Turn right with Chagrin River Road and cross bridge. Then turn left to stay on Chagrin River Road, which is also SR174
30.5	Cross Wilson Mills Road
32.9	Arrive at Squire's Castle Picnic Area

Emerald Necklace East

Ride begins at the Squire's Castle Picnic Area in North Chagrin Reservation on Chagrin River Road

0.0	Turn right out of Squire's Castle Picnic Area onto Chagrin River Road
2.4	Cross Wilson Mills Road
4.9	Turn right with Chagrin River Road and cross bridge. Then turn left to stay on Chagrin River Road,
9.9	Cross Polo Field
12.3	Cross Miles Road and bear left to continue on Chagrin River Road
12.4	Turn right onto Sulphur Springs Drive
13.1	Turn right onto Hawthorn Parkway
18.5	Turn left onto Richmond Road
18.8	Turn right onto Hawthorn Parkway
21.0	Cross Union Street and proceed onto Egbert Road
21.4	Turn right onto Gorge Parkway and enter Bedford Reservation
24.5	Cross Overlook Lane
25.6	Turn right onto Dunham Road
25.7	Turn left onto Tinkers Creek Road (Tinkers Creek Tavern is on the left side of Tinkers Creek Road shortly after the turn)
27.4	Turn left onto Canal Road
28.3	Exit Canal Road by exit ramp on left, up to Pleasant Valley Road/Alexander Road
28.4	Turn right onto Pleasant Valley Road
29.0	Turn left onto Brookside Road
29.1	Turn left onto Riverview Road
32.2	Cross Chippewa Road/SR82 and enter Brecksville Reservation
32.4	Turn right onto Chippewa Creek Drive
32.9	Turn left into Chippewa Picnic Area (or for dining, continue on Chippewa Creek Drive for 1.2 miles to Chippewa Road/SR82. Turn left. Restaurants on left are Simon's and the Courtyard; on the right are Panera Bread and Sakura's). Retrace route to start point

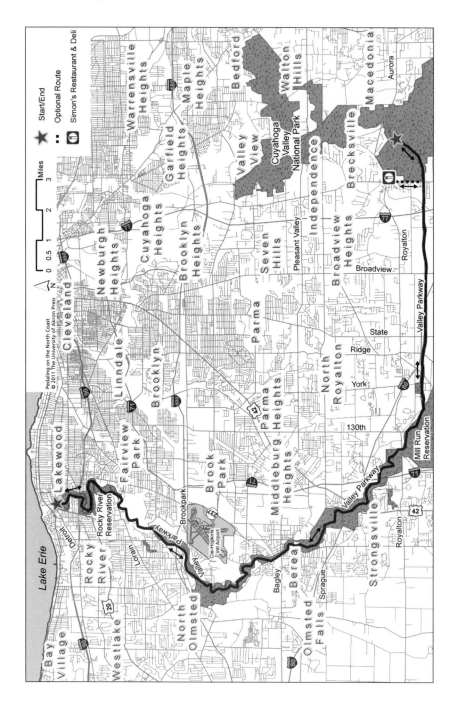